Aztecs in the American Southwest

by Humberto Garza

Aztecs in the American Southwest

Copyright (c) 2013
1st Edition
Author: Humberto Garza
Humbertogarza_2010@yahoo.com
http://www.joaquinmurrieta.net

Published by: Education and Leadership Press
4290 E. Ashlan Ave.
Fresno, CA 93726

Library of Congress Control Number: 2012954666
ISBN: 1-936209-10-1

Contributing Author and Copy Editor: Matt Espinoza Watson

Cover Design: Arturo Ríos

Editors: Paul Saindon, Dra. Elida G. Garza

First Printing of 1st Edition, February 2013

Printed and manufactured in the United States of America

Other books by the Humberto Garza:

Joaquín Murrieta, A Quest for Justice!

Joaquín, Demystifying the Murrieta Legend

The Mexican American War of 1846-1848, a Deceitful Smoke Screen

Organizing the Chicano Movement, the Story of CSO

Acknowledgements

Tlazokamatli (Thank you) to the following relatives: Víctor R. Garza and José Rolando Villarreal, who shared their private collection of books and other historical documents and who were very supportive of the research effort. Víctor and his young son (Eric) even took a special trip to the four corners area to explore the Aztec ruins. Without their information, patience, documentation, comments and suggestions, this work would not have been possible. The author is deeply indebted to them and Paul Saindon, my golfing friend, who volunteered to edit the work. Again, tlazokamatli (*gracias*) to all!

Other individuals whose prior meticulous research and field investigations made this book possible should be mentioned: Dr. Cecilio Orozco and Dr.Alfonso Rivas-Salmón who deciphered the Nahuatl writing on *El Libro del Sol* and made this book possible. The map research undertaken by Roberto Rodríguez and Patrisia Gonzales was outstanding as well, a valuable piece of the puzzle. Dr. Matt E. Watson, the copy editor and contributing author shared his photographs, research and writings on corn and movement *(ollin)*. And of course there are the American archaeologists whose published findings were also valuable pieces of the puzzle. I am deeply indebted to their research, work, and publications. Without their research and publications, the ancient history of the ancestors of the Chicanos, and the ancient history of the Mexicans in the United States, as well as the history of numerous Native American citizens would continue to be a mystery and/or intentionally omitted from our American History textbooks.

Contents

Preface

The work you are about to read has been a long time coming. It is a collection of incisive and critical questions and revolutionary ideas about the history of this land and the history of the indigenous people of the American Southwest.

I have been fascinated with the image of the *Piedra del Sol*, or *Tonalamatl*, since as long as I can remember. I have looked into it enough to know that nobody out there agrees on what it is, what it says, how it functions, or how to interpret all the symbols inscribed upon it. Beyond the twenty-day-signs ringing the central face of the calendar, academics, native elders, independent researchers, or novice interpreters of this historical artifact do not seem to agree among themselves or within their own respective group, much less with those from a different category or profession. Is the central face Tonatiuh or Tlaltecuhtli? Is the *tekpatl* (flint) tongue sticking out to demand human blood or to represent the dual power of our words to heal and to harm? Do the four quadrants around the central face represent locations, actual eras of time, mythological eras, or a combination of the three? From the *Museo de Antropología e Historia* in Mexico City to university libraries in California, books and people all seem to have different interpretations and answers of this ancient Aztec relic.

Having grown up in Fresno, and the son of two educators, I had heard of Dr. Cecilio Orozco very young in life, probably the first time I asked, "What does that thing mean?" when pointing at that dizzying haunting image of the Piedra del Sol. By the time I got to college at California State University at Fresno, Dr. Orozco had retired and was no longer offering his class or his summer field-trip, archaeological excursions into the four corners region of the American Southwest. But his name still came up, and it seemed that at least two generations of Chicanos in the Central San Joaquín Valley had learned about this stone from Dr. Orozco. Upon doing my own research, I quickly found out that what I knew about Dr. Orozco's theories on the meaning of this stone did not coincide with what was out there in the academic literature on the topic. I wondered about it but then promptly moved on with my life. It was not until years later, coming back to the San Joaquín Valley to begin teaching, that I met Ricardo Durán, a Chicano elder and founding member of the Raza Studies Program at Fresno State, and I was again exposed to intriguing ideas about that stone-calendar-sculpture. Even though Ricardo's own perspective differs from Dr. Cecilio Orozco, it was through Ricardo that I first met Dr. Orozco and got to listen to his unique and interesting perspective on this stone. A few years later, I met Humberto Garza when I was looking for someone to talk to about another elusive and mysterious subject, the life of Joaquín Murrieta. In the past three years, I have learned a great deal from Sr. Garza, and while I don't always agree with him, I respect his ideas and the work that he has done (and continues doing) tremendously.

I offer this preface as a disclaimer and as a dedication. The ideas presented within this text are just a beginning. The idea here is to start the discussion, to push others out there to ask important questions, and to do the research that needs to be done in order to more fully understand our past. The whole story may never be known, but what should be clear upon reading this book is that there is compelling evidence right in front of us that demands further investigation. In my eyes at least, Humberto Garza has done a great service to the legacies of Dr. Orozco and Dr. Rivas-Salmón since neither of them ever published an in-depth look at the evidence (which they uncovered) tying the Aztecs to the American Southwest. As those of you who know Humberto are aware that he is a unique and thought-provoking man. From upsetting conventional wisdom to helping organize communities to stand up for their rights, Humberto disrupts the status quo and is not the least bit timid about doing so. That being said, both Humberto and I invite you, the reader, to challenge the ideas put forth within this text and to help refine what we think we know about our past. As Humberto would say, "I am willing to learn; show me the evidence…"

Matt E. Espinoza Watson, J.D.
Instructor and Program Coordinator, Chicano-Latino Studies,
Fresno City College, Fresno, CA

The Five Suns of *El Libro del Sol*

The First Sun
Ce-Tonatiuh
Sun of Snow & Ice
Uknown - 1386 BC

This time period was known as a time of plenty, and was located north of the four corners area. Their Sun God sent snow and ice to cover their hunting grounds. The great herds disappeared, leaving behind only hungry predators that started to hunt and feed on humans, ending the time period.

The Second Sun
Ome Tonatiuh
Sun of Rain of Fire
1386 BC - 502 BC

Time period of the old, old, colorful land, and was located north of tenochtitlán where four rivers meet and the soil is red. A civilization based primarily on agriculture and supplemented by hunting, gathering, and trade. Time period was ended by a Rain of Fire, volcanic eruptions.

The Third Sun
Yei Tonatiuh
Sun of Wind
502 BC - 308 AD

Time period in the land of the egrets, and was located in *Culhuacan*, the place where the mountains curve. The area became known as Chicomostoc. Each valley had a river and farmland which could be irrigated, an abundance of birds, deer, and plenty of wild animals. Time period was ended by the Sun of Wind, tornadoes.

The Fourth Sun
Nahui Tomatiuh
Sun of Water
308 AD - 1325 AD

Time period in the land of deer, and was located on the coast of the *Oceano Pacifico* (Peaceful Ocean) in the community of Mazatlán. They prospered and developed a thriving community based on agriculture, hunting and fishing. Time period was ended by the Sun of Water, flooding and inundations.

The Fifth Sun
Macuilli Tonatiuh
Sun Near the Cactus
1325 AD - Present

Time Period started in Tenochtitlán, current day Mexico City. We are currently living in the fifth Sun, but do not know, when it would end.

An Introduction to the History of Mexican Americans in the United States

As American citizens of Mexican ancestry, we must claim our heritage and our history. As such, this work is an introduction to a piece of that history which is currently missing from American History textbooks. To proceed, we must first answer the following questions:

- When did Mexicans[1] first establish their residency in the North American continent?
- And when did their North American history begin?

Mexican Americans are citizens of the United States who are biologically, usually, a mixture of Native Americans and Spaniards or some other European country. Our *mestizaje* (mixture) also includes individuals with African and Asian ancestry though Spanish and Native cultures have historically been dominant in most areas of the American Southwest and in México[2]. Culturally, the vast majority of us are usually more Native than European, but we do have exceptions. A few of us are European in both culture and appearance while most of us are Native in appearance and culture – we range from one extreme to the other.

To answer the first question we need a time estimate as to when our Native ancestors populated the North American continent. So when did the first *homo sapiens* (wise people) come to the North American continent? Nobody really knows for sure. Scholars have a couple of theories, but these theories are really just suggestions at best. Until recently, very little scholarly research has been undertaken to qualify these ideas as legitimate theories. The most popular theory is that the first settlers in North America came from Asia trough the Bering Strait.

This theory states that people came to North American via

---

1   The term Mexican in this book will be used to refer to all residents of the United States who are descendants of citizens of México, whether resident immigrants or native born. As such, the term Mexican will include some people commonly called Hispanic, Latinos, Mexican Americans, Spanish Americans, Americans of Mexican descent, and some people who prefer to be called Indios, Indians. Citizens of México will be identified as Mexicanos.

2   For a more complete discussion of the term mestizaje as applied to Mexicans, read José Vasconcelos' book, *La Raza Cósmica*. He hypostasized that after all the "five" races in the world intermarry, their offsprings will look like Mexicans.

the Bering Straits when the ocean between the American and Asian continents was frozen at the time. Scientists estimate that this migration occurred between 13,000 and 15,000 years ago. According to this theory, Asians walked across because they were following the game animals that had crossed before them. Before the 1980s, very limited scholarly research actually existed to qualify this idea as a theory. What we did have was a lot of individuals repeating the same idea over and over and over again but with very little actual research to back up their assumption. We know that archaeologists have found human remains and human made artifacts which led these scholars to believe that human beings resided in North America at least 13,000 to 15,000 years ago or maybe even earlier.

There are other theories about how the North and South American continents became inhabited. For example, some scholars have suggested that people might have come to North America from South America. In Perú, archaeological evidence indicated that a certain region in South America, where the Moche Natives civilization flourished, might have been settled by Polynesians, or at least that the Moche Natives were visited by Polynesians who sailed across the Pacific Ocean directly into South America. The reason for this suggestion was that the artifacts found in Moche Natives cities bare a strong resemblance to Polynesian artifacts, especially the clothing, pottery, and fishing nets. According to these scholars, the similarities are astounding. However, the earliest archaeological findings of the Moche Natives in South America to date indicate their civilization existed at least 6,500 years ago, possibly as early as 4500 B.C. According to this hypothesis, the Moche, or their predecessors, could have landed in South America and their descendants could have then traveled to Central America and years later into North America.

In Puma Punku, Bolivia, South America, an archaeological site discovered a long time ago and that has been pillaged for centuries is now being studied by archeologists. They believe this site to have been built around 17000 B.C. These archeologists also noted that the stone structures constructed by the Natives would be extremely difficult to build today even with our modern tools and technology.

Also, in the 1980s an archeologist established the existence of human beings in the Americas as early as 32,000 years ago. The findings of this archaeological site were published in the scientific journal *Nature* and stated, "Archaeologist Niede Guidon summed up her finding in the title: 'Carbon-14 dates point to man in the Americas 32,000 years ago.' Niede Guidon's findings were based on archaeological evidence found in Brazil."[3] Another archaeological site found at Monte Verde in Chile yielded information and artifacts about a civilization that were originally radiocarbon dated to roughly 14,000 years ago.

According to archaeologists, in the year 11000 B.C. in the State of New México, a civilization known as the "Clovis people" settled in and around the community of Clovis, New México.[4] We know that archaeologists have also found similar artifacts in Fowler, New México, which indicates a civilization established their residence in that area around 9000 B. C. Another North American archaeological discovery, "The Meadowcroft Rockshelter in Pennsylvania, yielded artifacts that were originally dated using radiocarbon to roughly 16,000 to 19,000 years ago, pre-dating Clovis by 5,000 years or more."[5] In 2002, an archaeologist from the University of Oregon's Museum of Natural and Cultural History found human fossilized excrement (coprolites) and other artifacts at Paisley Caves in the State of Oregon. DNA testing of the coprolites established they were human excretion and radiocarbon dating placed the coprolites at 14,300 years old, more than 1,000 years older than the Clovis findings.

The existence of the Moche Natives in Perú, the Clovis people in New México, the civilization in Fowler, New México, the Meadowcroft Rockshelter in Pennsylvania, the fossilized excrement

3   Wells, Spencer. 2002. *The Journey of Man, A Genetic Odyssey* (Princeton University Press, 41 William Street, Princeton, New Jersey), p.137.
4   The artifacts were discovered near the community of Clovis, New México, hence the name, "Clovis people."
5   Ibid, p. 136.

found in Paisley Caves in Oregon, and the archaeological site in Monte Verde are well within the range of the time period proposed by the Bering Straits Theory 13,000 to 15,000 years ago. However, Puma Punku and the Niede Guidon archaeological finding in Brazil, at least one DNA study, and other archaeological findings strongly suggest an earlier crossing of Asian settlers into the North and South American continents. Guidon's archaeological site in Brazil could be 33,000 years old, while in México, they discovered footprints, which might be even older than Guidon's findings.

In a scientific study authored by Spencer Wells in the book, **The Journey of Man, A Genetic Odyssey**, he wrote, *"...the male Y-chromosome has been used to trace the spread of humanity from Africa into Eurasia and then into North America and South America, and why differing racial types emerged when mountain ranges split population groups, and that the San Bushman of the Kalahari [Africa] have some of the oldest genetic markers in the world. We learn, finally with certainty, that Neanderthals are not our ancestors and that the entire genetic diversity of Native Americans can be accounted for by just ten individuals."*[6] Furthermore, from this scientific study we learn that these Eurasian people could have crossed into North America as early as 50,000 years ago. In this study, the spread of the Y-chromosome (M-130) lineages suggests that these human beings could have arrived in the North American continent as early as 50,000 years ago, and a later crossing of human being labeled as the M3 lineages came about 10,000 years ago.[7] In this study, the author suggests that these first Americans could have reached the southern most tip of South America (*Tierra del Fuego, Chile*) within 1,000 years after their initial arrival on the North American continent (about 49,000 years ago).

In Mexico City in the *Museo Nacional de Antropología e Historia*, the National Museum of Anthropology and History, as one enter the museum, a glass platform, about 20 feet wide and 20 feet long and about 3 feet high, covers a cavity, which is about 6 feet deep. As one approaches the glass-viewing platform, the visitor can

6   Ibid, cover folder.
7   Ibid, p.182-3

see a skeleton of a mammoth with two giant tusks at the bottom of the cavity.

Upon closer examination, underneath the mammoth's bones lays the skeleton of a human being. According to the museum authorities, carbon dating tests performed on the mammoth and the human bones date these remains to be at least 11,000 years old. This means that in 9000 B.C., mammoths and human beings lived in the Valley of Anahuac, near present-day Mexico City. This discovery implies that human beings have lived in the Valley of Anahuac for well over 11,000 years, and we have no written history on these human beings. The earliest Native civilization recorded in México are the *Ulmecatl* (or at least this is what the Aztecs, who were around some two thousand years later, knew them by; they are common-

ly known as the Olmec.), but their civilization is believed to have begun around 1000 B.C. There is a gap of 8,000 years between the mammoth hunters in the Anahuac Valley and the beginning of the Olmec civilization. What happened in between these 8,000 years?

In 1954, the skeletons of the mammoth and of the human artifacts were unearthed by construction workers digging near the town of Santa Isabel Iztapan, a small community located northeast of downtown Mexico City. During the excavation the workers accidently uncovered the skel-etons on what used to be the an-

Photograph by Dr. Matt Espinoza Watson at the *Museo Nacional de Antropología e Historia.* My thanks to Professor Espinoza Watson for the use of this photograph.

cient shore of Lake Texcoco in 9000 B.C. The authorities quickly halted the digging, carefully removed the bones, and preserved the skeletons which are now one of the main exhibits at the National Museum of Anthropology and History in Mexico City.

Photograph by Dr. Matt Espinoza Watson taken at the the *Museo Nacional de Antropología e Historia*, in Mexico City. According to the display the hunter in the corner, right-center, is the one who got too close to spear the mammoth in the heart, and the animal fell on top of him.

According to carbon dating tests performed on these skeletons, the archaeologists believe that human beings lived in the Valley of Anahuac about 11,000 years ago, and apparently these human beings were hunting mammoths as well[8]. The museum's display suggests that a hunter got too close to a wounded mammoth to spear him in the heart, thereby killing the animal. In the process of killing the mammoth, the wounded animal fell on top of the hunter.

After the mammoth was killed, the other companions took whatever meat they could carry and left the dead hunter where he was accidently killed. At the time, the hunting companions had no

8   Mammoths are believed to have gone extinct in the North American continent around 10000 B.C., but apparently their estimate is off by at least a thousand years.

16

means available to lift the dead mammoth so they could recover his remains. As such, they left their hunting partner where he was accidently squashed to death. This information pre-dates the existence of human beings in México by at least 8,000 years before the first great Mesoamerican civilization in México as perceived by some "authorities of Pre-Columbian History," such as Charles Phillips, author of *The Complete Illustrated History of the Aztec & Mayas.*[9]

In 2007, archaeologist Silva González from Liverpool John Moore's University, in the United Kingdom uncovered 325 indentations in a quarry, which later proved to be animal and human footprints. The archaeologist found this quarry and the footprints on *Cerro Toluquillo,* a volcanic mountain basin in Valsequillo near the City of Puebla in the State of Puebla, México.

According to the archaeologists involved in this study, *"Prehistoric people and some animals walked in soft damp volcanic ash along a lakeshore shortly after a volcanic eruption. The ash later hardened into rock preserving the footprints."*[10]   By dating the soil layers above the footprints, the soil of the indentions, and the soil below the footprints, *"the daters of these footprints suggest that these footprints were made about 40,000 years ago."* [11]

This photo copy of the animal and the human footprints was taken from http:llwww.mexicanfootprints.co.uk/research/location.htm

Niede Guidon's archaeological finding in Brazil is approximately 25,000 to 40,000 years old, and the findings in the quarry in Pueblo, México, are much older than the Bering Strait Theory's time period, which suggests that human beings first crossed the frozen

9   Phillips, Charles. *The Complete Illustrated History of the Aztec & Maya* (Hermes House: Printed in Singapore).

10   *National Geographic News*, February 23, 2007. http://news.nationalgeographic.com/news/2008/06/080606-ancient-footprints.html

11   *National Geographic News*, Reporting Your World Daily, "Footprints Show 1st Americans Came 25,000 Years Earlier," December 2, 2009.

Photograph by Matt Espinoza Watson taken at the *Museo Nacional de Antropología e Historia*, in Mexico City. According to this display ancient human beings in the Anahuac Valley lived and socialized as suggested in 9000 B.C.

sea/land bridge between Asia and Alaska about 13,000 to 15,000 years ago. We need a much earlier time estimate to explain these findings.

To answer the second question, as to when the history of Chicanos[12] in the United States begins, first we must realize that American History as taught today often intentionally omits the existence and the contributions of these people as well as the history of other non-white Americans. As an example of such an omission we offer the archeological findings of the human and mammoth skeletons uncovered in Mexico City, which are over 11,000 years old. This means that human beings lived in the North American continent for thousands of years before Columbus "discovered that human beings were already living in America."

---

12   Throughout the book the term Chicano will be used interchangeably to refer to American citizens of Mexican descent. Historically, the term Chicano has several origins, according to which one you adhere to. For example, *Don* Alfredo Figueroa, President of the International Association of Joaquin Murrieta Descendants, offers a unique explanation for this term. "The term Chicano did not start with the Chicano movement in the 1960's or the 70's. Centuries before, the Aztecs used the term Chix-Zanotl to mean vanguard – vanguard of their treasures. Gradually over time the term evolved to Chicano. And the term kept re-appearing, for example in 1810, when Miguel Hidalgo started the movement to become independent from Spain, he used the name of 'Los Chicanos;' a hundred years later, in 1910, Emiliano Zapata's main escorts were called 'Los Chicanos' as well."

As another example of an extremely important historical omission from American History, we offer the historical information contained in *El Libro del Sol*, The Book of the Sun, which was also uncovered in downtown Mexico City in 1760, and finally deciphered and translated into the Spanish language in 1965, by Dr. Alfonso Rivas-Salmón from the *Universidad Autónoma de Guadalajara*. According to Dr. Rivas-Salmón's interpretation, this archaeological relic, a history book written in stone, contains the historical data which establishes the presence of one of the ancestors of the Mexicans, the Aztecs, as residents in the four corners area of the American Southwest in the year 1386 B.C., over 3,300 years ago. As such, *El Libro de Sol*, one of the few indigenous books not destroyed by the conquering Europeans, contains precious and priceless American History – for all Americans but especially for Native Americans, Mexicans and their descendants.

As stated, pertinent historical information is often omitted from our textbooks, sometimes intentionally, other times due to ignorance. Secondly, often, the historians are not familiar with the history of the first Americans, and nor are they well versed on the history of the Native American civilizations such as the Toltecs, Chichimecas, the Aztecs, and all Native Americans who at earlier times resided in the American Southwest and whose descendants still reside in the United States. At other times historical facts are known and then intentionally omitted, mislabeled, misinterpreted, or their significance is marginalized.[13]

For example, the archaeological findings in the American Southwest, which American archaeologists have, for whatever reason for decades, classified and identified as "Anasazi ruins" are indisputably linked to the civilizations of ancient México. These so-called "Anasazi ruins" could be the ancient ruins of the Toltec, the Chichimecas, or the Aztec civilizations in the American Southwest.

---

13   As another example of intentional omission of American historical facts we offer the following: During the American Revolution 3,000 Mexican soldiers from the State of Oaxaca, and 3,000 soldiers from the island of Santiago de Cuba fought at the Battle of Yorktown alongside the American rebels. This invaluable American History information is intentionally omitted. I often wondered if General George Washington required these 6,000 Hispanic soldiers to speak "English only," before they could fight and die for America's independence.

We call these ruins "Aztec" because according to written Aztec history, their civilization flourished in the heart of the American Southwest, the four corners area, from 1386 B.C. to 502 B.C, a total of 884 years. Their descendants who chose to remain behind later became known as the Hopi, Pueblo, Yaqui, Shoshoni, Ute, Piute, Comanche, Zuni, Acoma, and others Native American nations, which still reside in the American Southwest.

The four corners area consists of the territories where the current borders of four present-date western states, Utah, Arizona, New México, and Colorado meet and form four corners. According to documented Aztec history, this was the second ancient homeland of the Aztecs in the North American continent. *The Book of the Sun* establishes their residence in the four corners area in the year 1386 B.C. According to this book their first ancient homeland was further north, but they abandoned these northern hunting grounds because the great herds had disappeared with the coming of an ice age. In the year 1386 B.C., the ancestors of the Aztecs settled in southern Utah, on the Green River basin, close to the area where the Green River and the Colorado River meet, and for 884 years they resided in the area. As their civilization grew in numbers and size, they expanded their settlements from southern Utah into northern and southern Arizona, and into southern Colorado, then into New México, and even into what we know today as Oklahoma, Texas, and the States of Chihuahua and Sonora, México. They created a civilization based on agriculture which extended from the Green River basin in Utah to an area covering well over 500,000 square miles with numerous farming villages, cities which had four and five story high buildings, cliff dwellings, public buildings, ball courts, dams, irrigation canals, and numerous ceremonial sites. An improved 30-foot wide road connected all these villages. Their descendants, with time, even constructed a ceremonial center and a university in Pueblo Bonito, New México, and a four-story high observatory for studying the movement and behavior of astronomical objects in Casa Grande, Arizona.

Based on the numerous archaeological sites found and uncovered in the four corners area, a conservative estimate of the Aztec population in the year 502 B.C. could be approximately 700,000 to well over a million people. However, for some unknown reason to the modern archaeologists, and to American historians, most of these ancient Native Americans abandoned their homeland, their cities and villages and departed south seeking a new beginning, but some stayed behind. Today, the descendants of these previously "unknown" Native Americans refer to this ancient homeland of the Aztecs in the American Southwest as the heart of Aztlán. And while we still do not know for sure when the first *homo sapiens* arrived in the North American continent, we do know for certain that the Aztecs settled the four corners area of the United States in the year 1386 B.C. As such and as the descendants of the Aztecs, the Chicanos and the Mexican Americans can claim a recorded history and a presence in the United States of America that is close to 3,300 years old. Recently (these past decades), uninformed European immigrants whose ancestors have been in the North American continent less then 300 years erroneously refer to these Aztec descendants as "illegal aliens," as if these Native North Americans had come from outer space.

Chapter I: *El Libro del Sol*, The Book of the Sun

We do not know when the *Mexica* (Aztec) first settled the North American continent. Nor do we know for certain when the first people came to the continent. We do know that the Mexica recorded a portion of their history in the *Libro del Sol* which states that they resided in the four corners area of the American Southwest from 1386 B.C. to 502 B.C.. The Mexicas and their descendants have resided in present-day United States territory for over 3,300 years[14]. The Mexicas are one of the ancestors of the Mexican Americans who reside in the United States today. As such, these Mexicas resided on this continent for thousands of years before their descendents mated with the few Spaniards who landed on the shores of some North America island by mistake and years later, finally landed on Mexican territory.

In 1492, these "discoverers of America" were lost at sea searching for a western passage to India. They accidently landed on an island off the North American continent. We know that the Spanish ancestors of the Mexican Americans, as documented by numerous American historians, first landed on a Caribbean island on October 12, 1492. The Spaniards, believing they had reached India, labeled the indigenous population "Indians." The indigenous *Tainos* or Arawa were happy to feed these lost, hungry strangers. We do not know for certain when the North American Natives, the primary ancestors of the Chicanos[15], first come to the North American continent?

El Libro del Sol (The Book of the Sun) is one of the oldest recorded histories of the Aztecs. This history book, carved in stone, contains a portion of the history of the Aztecs as recorded by Aztecs. The four specific time periods documented in the book begin in the year 1386 B.C., the year the first Aztec time period ends and

14   And some people erroneously label us "new immigrants" to the United States, and sometimes they even refer to us as "illegal aliens" in our homeland.

15   Chicano is a term used primarily by Mexican Americans. As such, most Chicanos are usually part Native Americans and part Spaniard. However, as a rule, Chicanos are more Native than Spanish simply because of the numbers. There were at least 25 to 50 million American Natives in what became *Nueva España*, New Spain, and about 100,000 Spaniards; a ratio of about one Spaniard for every 500 Natives. Because of sickness brought over by the Spaniards, millions of Native Americans died. By 1620 or so, it is estimated that the native population in México declined to about 1,000,000, but this would still be a ratio of 10 Native Americans to 1 European. How Spanish can we be?

23

Painting by Arturo Ríos

The circular figure above is known by several names, such as *El Libro del Sol*, The Book of the Sun, *El Calendario Azteca*, The Aztec Calendar, the *Tonalamatl*, The Record of the Passing of the Days of the Sun, and *La Piedra del Sol*, The Stone of the Sun. None of these names provide a clue as to what this Aztec artifact really is. It is a historical document carved in stone. In short, it is a history book which records the history of the Aztecs in the American Southwest. This artifact records the years and the locations of the Aztec's former residencies before they finally settled in *Tenochtitlán* (Mexico City) in 1325 A.D.

the 2nd time period begins. The historical information recorded on *El Libro del Sol* ends in the year 1325 A.D., at the end of the 4th time period, and at the beginning of the 5th time period. The 5th time period, called *El Quito Sol*, is the epoch we are currently living today. This history book records the residency of the Aztecs in the American Southwest during their second time period [1386 B.C. to 502 B.C.]. As such, we offer this documented history of the Aztecs, who created a civilization and resided in the American Southwest, as a means of assisting American historians in filling the huge void in American History as it relates to American citizens, especially to the Native Americans and their descendants.

El libro del Sol was written in Aztec literary terms. According to Professor Cecilio Orozco, an expert on the history of the Aztecs and who retired from California State University at Fresno, the term "Nahuatl, means the four great waters," *nahui*, four, *atl*, water[16]. This historical relic documents the fact that the Aztecs settled the four corners area of the American Southwest in the year 1386 B.C. It follows, then, that at least one of the North American Native Nations, ancestors of the Chicanos, lived in what is now the American Southwest at least 3,396 years ago [as of 2010]. Consequently, Mexicans and Chicanos can claim at least 3,396 years of recorded residency in the United States.

This chronology provides the Chicanos the historical evidence of their ancestors' written history that is at least 3,396 years old and of their ancestors' residency in the United States of America predating 1386 B.C. This history of the ancestors of the Chicanos, the Aztecs, is a "written history" of the oldest civilization in the American Southwest. Chicanos and Mexican Americans can claim 3,396 years of residency in the United States of America, even if today we cannot find this American History recorded in current history textbooks.

As stated earlier, our other ancestors, the Europeans, landed on a Caribbean Island on October 12, 1492, a date some historians refer to as Columbus Day. In Latin American countries, historians refer to this date as *El Día de la Raza,* The Day of the Race. Why? Because on that day, a Spaniard and an American Native mated and nine months later gave birth to a *mestizo*, a half-breed child. As far as we know, before October 12, 1492, not one person (*mestizo*), half Spanish and half Native American, had ever been conceived. Consequently, to Chicanos, October 12, 1492, denotes the date a new race was conceived (half Native, half European). We celebrate that date not as Columbus Day, but as the birth date of what we call *La*

---

16   Orozco, Cecilio, *The Book of the Sun, Tonatiuh,* 2nd Edition, California State University, Fresno, California, 1992, p. 17. The four great waters are the Green, Colorado, Escalante, and San Juan Rivers which meet to form one river, the Colorado.

Raza, The Race[17]. In the eyes of *"Latinos"* from countries in North America, South America, and Central America, the creation of a new race of people, just like them, certainly warrants a celebration far surpassing the celebration of the arrival of uninvited, lost sailors landing on a foreign island by mistake.

El Libro del Sol (The Book of the Sun) is a massive history book that stands nearly 12 feet tall and 3 feet thick. It weights approximately 25 tons. It is a significant historical artifact, which currently stands in the *Museo de Antropología e Historia* in Mexico City. To the delight of some North American historians, this artifact has been deciphered and translated into the Spanish language. At least two academicians know this relic contains a significant portion of the recorded history of the Aztecs. These academicians refer to *El Libro del Sol*, or the Aztec Calendar if you will, as the **Book of Tonatiuh**[18].

Tonatiuh is the name of the Aztec's Sun God. These two historians, Dr. Cecilio Orozco from California State University at Fresno and Dr. Alfonso Rivas-Salmón from the *Universidad Autónoma de Guadalajara*, Jalisco, México, know this history book contains a portion of the documented history of the Mexica[19], meaning "the people of the sun."

---

17   As previously stated, Chicanos are mostly Native and European. As such, Chicanos have white and black ancestors because of their Spanish blood. The Spaniards were conquered and occupied by the Moors (792 to 1492) for 700 years, and our Native mothers were former Asian immigrates. As such, Chicanos ancestors were white, black, yellow, and red people. In his book José Vasconcelos referred to us as "La Raza Cosmica." Vasconcelos hypothesized that when all the humans on earth eventually intermarry, their off springs will look just like Chicanos.

18   Orozco, Cecilio, 1983, 1992, 2nd Edition, *The Book of the Sun, Tonatiuh*, Fresno State University, Fresno, California.

19   *Mexicas*, this term has several meanings, depending upon who you ask. A linguist claims this nahuatl word means, "son of the maguey." Alfonso Caso and other anthropologists have interpreted this name to mean, "those who reside in the middle/bellybutton of the lake of the moon," as Lake Texcoco, where the Mexica built their capital city, was referred to as the lake of the moon (meztli). Others have hypothesized that the name comes from the prophet Mexitli, who led the people out of Aztlán and into MéxicoCity, Tenochtitlán; and some say that Mexitli or Mexi was another name that was used for Huitzilopochtli, the primary deity of the Mexica. A historian claims Mexica means "those that worship the sun." A Mexicano told me that as a child he was taught [in Mexico City's public schools] that "Mejica" was the Aztecs' war cry. Whenever they went into battle they would shout "Mejica! Mejica!," meaning "I am ready to die, for to die in combat was the greatest honor an Aztec warrior could earn. Other Native tribes referred to the Aztecs as "Mejicas."

Recorded in *El Libro del Sol* it is the history of four epochs, four specific time periods, each lasting hundreds of years. Each epoch was ended by a natural catastrophe. According to the Aztecs these natural disasters were Tonatiuh's way of ordering them to leave the area they inhabited at the time. Each of these natural calamities caused great upheaval and devastation to the Aztecs and to their communities. The Aztecs referred to the time period between disasters as a *sol,* a sun, or an epoch. For example, after the 4th catastrophe, upon the completion of the 4th Sun, the Aztecs, led by Chief Tenoch migrated into the Valley of Anahuac. There they

A painting by Jesús Enrique Emilio de la Helguera Espinoza for the *Cigarrera La Moderna, S.A. de C.V.* This painting illustrates Helguera's artistic representation of the founding of Tenochtitlán. This representation could be found in numerous calendars in México and in the American Southwest in the 1940s, 1950s, and 1960s. According to legend the Aztecs were searching for a new homeland, and as instructed by their God, they were to settle this new land wherever they found an eagle perched on a cactus, devouring a serpent.

established *Tenochtitlán*, currently known as Mexico City.

This historical relic, *El Libro del Sol*, records that the Aztec

Nation had lived four suns and experienced four major catastrophes before they finally arrived in the Valley of Anahuac. After several generations of living in the Valley of Anahuac in the year 1325 A.D., the Aztecs decided to build their permanent home on an island.

Once in the Valley of Anahuac, the Aztecs started to live the next epoch, the 5th sun, on the island city they named *Tenochtitlán*. This island was located in the middle of Lake Texcoco in the heart of the Anahuac Valley, a beautiful valley surrounded by mountains. Chicanos, as well as Aztecs, refer to our current epoch as *el quinto sol*, the 5th sun, which started in the year 1325 A.D. According to the Aztec myth and to the Mayan legend, this epoch may end on December 21, 2012.

According to Dr. Cecilio Orozco, the 7.8 earthquakes, which occurred in Mexico City in the year 1985, signaled the beginning of the end of the 5th sun time period, and the imminent coming of the 6th sun. According to this Aztec historian, we should be starting the *sexto sol*, the 6th sun, very shortly. Also, according to Dr. Orozco, it was prophesized by the Aztecs that during the 6th sun, the descendents of the Aztecs will once again gain control of their environment. They will become prosperous and more humane. They will, once again, be in control of their own destiny.

Carved at the very left top-center portion of the *El Libro del Sol,* you will find a figure, which contains an acatl. *Acatl,* means *caña* in Spanish, a cane or reed in English. In this cartouche, the cane, centered in the middle of the cartouche represents the 13th day of the month in the Aztec calendar. The complete cartouche establishes the date the Book of the Sun was completed, dedicated, and presented to the Aztec emperor Axayacatl (1469-1481). A person wishing to decode the complete cartouche on the left must engage in a simple exercise of basic logic. The symbol in the middle represents a cane, or acatl, and is surrounded by 13 circles. Each circle represents the number one; therefore, we have 13 *acatl.* According to Dr. Rivas-Salmón and Dr. Orozco, in the aztec language, the year 13 acatl translates into the year 1479 A.D. According to both

historians, this history book carved in stone was completed in the year 1479 A.D. We also know from recorded Aztec history that Axayacatl was the *tlatoani* (literally "speaker"), or ruler, of the Aztec Empire at the time.

The authors consolidated and summarized historical codices and condensed the entire written history of the Aztecs. Consequently, the previous four suns and the history of these time periods were engraved onto this amazing history book. Once completed, *El Libro del Sol* was publically displayed in the main plaza in *Tenochtitlán,* from 1479 to 1521. This public educational project provided the citizens of the Aztec Empire, especially the children, the opportunity to read and to learn the history of their ancestors.

In 1521, forty-two (42) years after the Book of the Sun was completed, and during the battle for *Tenochtitlán* and the conquest of the Aztec empire, the Aztecs intentionally buried *El Libro del Sol* before the Spaniards and their numerous Native allies could destroy it. Shortly thereafter, the other Native nations and their Spanish allies soundly defeated the Aztecs.

The Libro del Sol is read from the middle out. In the middle is *Tonatiuh*, the Sun God, representing the current time period, *El Quito Sol*, The Fifth Sun, surrounded by the four cartouches which represent the four great catastrophes which ended each *sol*. The 1st Sun was the Sun of the Jaguar, cartouche on the top right corner. The 2nd Sun was the Sun of Rain of Fire, bottom left cartouche. The 3rd Sun was the Sun of Wind, cartouche on the top left corner. The 4th Sun was the Sun of Water, the cartouche on the bottom right corner represents this time period. After the 4th Sun, the Aztecs started the 5th Sun in *Tenochtitlán*. We are currently living in the 5th Sun time period, and this epoch has yet to be written. It may end on December 21, 2012, as prophesied.

After the battle, the Book of the Sun remained buried for 239 years. In 1760, it was accidently unearthed during a major construction project in downtown Mexico City.

The construction workers who uncovered this historic relic were digging a foundation for a new building when they encountered a gigantic rock covered with symbols. The massive rock, *El Libro del Sol*, was lifted, removed, cleaned, and then stored in the backyard of the local Catholic cathedral. The stone was leaned against the back outer wall of the cathedral, and there it stood, unprotected from the elements for 225 years, until 1885. During this time period, because the twenty (20) symbols for each day in the

30

The first outer circle around Tonatiuh's face contains 20 symbols. Each symbol represents a day in the Aztec calendar. Because of these twenty symbols, when this historical stone was found, people believed it was an "Aztec Calendar." For example, in this circle the top green and white cartouche with a red circle represents the day of *xochitl*, the day of the flower, the 20th day of the month.

Aztec calendar were already known, the Mexican citizens referred to this relic as *El Calendario Azteca*, The Aztec Calendar.

When this historical artifact was first uncovered, 239 years after the brutal conquest of the Aztecs, most Mexican citizens could no longer speak their native tongue, *Nahautl*, much less identify the Aztec symbols and their meaning. By 1760, when the relic was uncovered, most Mexicans spoke the language of their conquerors, *Español* (Spanish), as had been mandated and enforced sadistically by the Spanish authorities. The few Aztecs who spoke Nahuatl could no longer decode the meaning of the symbols in the Book of the Sun. Therefore, the vast majority of the Mexicans could not

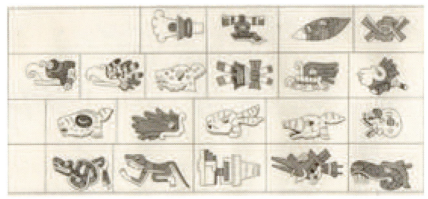

The 20 days of the Aztec month are represented on the right, starting at the bottom right hand corner, reading right to left, with the 1st day of the month, *cipactli* (cayman), *ehecatl* (wind), *calli* (house), *cuetzpalin* (lizard), *coatl* (serpent), *miquiztli* (death), *mazatl* (deer), *tochtli* (rabbit), *atl* (water), *itzcuintli* (dog), *ozomatli* (monkey), *malinalli* (weed), *acatl* (reed), *ocelot*l (ocelot), *cuauhtli* (eagle), *cozcacuahtli* (vulture), *ollin* (movement), *tecpatl* (obsidian), *quiahuitl* (rain), and the last day of the month, the 20th day of the month, *xochitl* (flower).

easily decode the written history carved in this stone, but they could readily identify the symbols of the 20 days of the Aztec calendar. Consequently, they believed *El Libro del Sol* was a calendar. Even today very few *Mexicanos* know it is a recorded history.

In 1965, Dr. Rivas-Salmón from *La Universidad Autónoma de Guadalajara*, in the State of Jalisco, México, a law professor whose leisure pursuit is Aztec History, deciphered the writings on *El Libro del Sol*.

In 1982, Dr. Orozco, a native of California, who was later teaching at the School of Education at CSU Fresno, in California, working independently, also deciphered *El Libro del Sol*.

Dr. Orozco refers to the Aztec Calendar as *The Book of Tonatiuh*, the book of their Sun God. Both university professors, Dr. Orozco and Dr. Rivas-Salmón, learned the Nahuatl language before they could decipher the carvings on the stone. In 1990, Dr. Orozco, once again joined forces with Dr. Rivas-Salmón to compared notes. The collaborators realized they had arrived at the same conclusions independently.

These two scholars discovered, based on the deciphered information in the *Libro del Sol*, that the Aztecs lived in the American Southwest over 2,500 years before Columbus landed in America. These Native Americans resided in the land the Chicanos refer to as *Aztlán,* the land of the egrets, a place to the north of Tenochtitlán [Mexico City] where four rivers meet and where the soil is red. Additionally, they discovered information leading them to believe that the Aztecs were probably the ancestors of several Native American tribes currently residing in the American Southwest. As stated, the historical information recorded in *El Libro del Sol* relates that the Aztec's ancient homeland was a place up north where four great rivers met, and where the soil was red. Consequently, each scholar started searching for such a geographical location and both, independently of each other concluded the only such geographical location existed in the four corners area of the American Southwest.

As a young man Dr. Orozco worked as a teacher and later as a principal in the Native American reservations in New Méxi-

"The face of *Tonatiuh*, represents the Aztec's Sun God, in the center of *El Libro del Sol*. The Aztecs believed that *Tonatiuh* needed nourishment to fight the darkness during the night and to be strong enough to re-appear the next day. Therefore, the two figures on both sides of *Tonatiuh* have a human heart in their mouth, *Tonatiuh's* nourishment. In Aztec culture, "these blood sacrifices have a three-fold function; it creates the world, it sustains it, and as it sustains it, transforms it. The Aztecs were obsessed by the responsibility for keeping the cosmos in movement. They believed that the universe is in eternal danger of stopping, and thus perishing. To avoid this catastrophe man must nourish the sun with his blood."[1]

---

1   Paz, Octavio, 1990. *México, Splendors of Thirty Centuries*, "Will for Form," (A Bulfinch Press Book: The Metropolitan Museum of Art, New York), p.12.

co. During this time, he had opportunities to scout for artifacts in the Aztec ruins located in the surrounding areas. Years later, while teaching at Fresno State University, he invited his former teacher and friend, Dr. Rivas-Salmón to join him in the exploration of the four corners area. These two scholars located the four rivers indicated in the history book: the Colorado, the San Juan, the Escalante, and the Green Rivers[20]. Several smaller rivers in the area were also found to contain numerous artifacts and Aztec ruins. The soil surrounding the area where the four rivers meet is red. These four main rivers join together to form the robust Río Colorado.[21] This river continues its flow west and south across the American Southwest and empties into the Sea of Córtez in Baja California, México.

Together, they walked the American Southwest in search of archaeological evidence of habitation by the Aztecs. They explored the four corners area where the four rivers actually meet and the soil is red. This is the only place in the United States where four states' borders meet and form four corners. *El Libro del Sol* identifies this location as the ancient homeland of the Aztecs and the place where they settled after abandoning their ancient homeland located further north. This migration occurred because of an ice age, the first catastrophe noted as the end of *el primer sol*, the 1st sun. As recorded in the Book of the Sun, the Aztecs arrived in the four corners area to begin *El Segundo Sol* (the 2nd sun) in the year 1386 B.C.
.
THE FIRST SUN: TIME OF PLENTY

According to Dr. Rivas-Salmón and Dr. Orozco, recorded in The Book of *Tonatiuh*, the Aztec Nation lived *El Primer Sol*, the 1st Sun, in a land further north of the four corners area. The land nurtured great herds of animals, which provided a stable diet of meat and clothing. They referred to this northern land as their hunting grounds. This time period is known as *El Primer Sol*, the 1st sun, a

---

20   Dr. Cecilio Orozco believes that the four rivers were the Green River, the Colorado River, and the San Juan River and that the fourth river was the one formed by these 3 rivers. The three rivers did create a much larger Colorado River.
21   In 1540, Francisco Vásquez de Coronado, guided by Hopi, explored the American Southwest for the Spanish crown. He named the river El Río Colorado, now known as the Colorado River. In the Spanish language El Río Colorado means the "The Colored River."

34

Ocelotonatiuh, Sol del Jaguar, Sun of the Jaguar, in the cartouche the symbol of the cat represents the predators that were feeding upon the people at the end of the 1st sol. The snow and ice caused the great herds to depart, and the predators started to hunt human beings. This ice age and the predators caused the Aztecs to leave their northern hunting grounds in the year 1386 B.C. They moved south, into the four corners area and arrived the same year, 1386 B.C. According to weather historians, this area of northwestern United States experienced an Ice Age around 1400 B.C. (Not bad, the weather historians' time estimation was off by 14 years.).

time of plenty.

Also, recorded in the Book of the Sun, the Aztecs lived a very happy life in the northern homeland until 1386 B.C. According to the recorded legend, *Tonatiuh*, the Aztec sun God, decided his people should leave. *Tonatiuh* sent snow and ice to cover their hunting grounds. The great herds disappeared, leaving behind only hungry predators that started to hunt and feed on humans.

In 1990, the two academicians, during their exploration of the four corners area, found numerous Aztec artifacts and petro glyphs which shed additional light on the history of the area and reinforced their translation of the documented history in *El Libro del Sol*. The petro glyphs and artifacts verified that the Aztec Nation lived in the four corners area during *El Segundo Sol*, The 2nd Sun, [from 1386 B.C. to 502 B.C.]. This period ended with another catastrophe, *El Sol de Lluvia de Fuego*, the Sun of Rain of Fire, which started in the year 502 B.C.

We do not know when the 1st Sun time period begin. The Aztecs probably had not yet developed a calendar, or a method for keeping track of time. They were, therefore, unable to record the date of the beginning of the 1st sun period. We do know when it ended. The 1st sun epoch ended in the year 1386 B.C. in the same year the Aztecs arrived at the four corners area.[22] During the 800 plus years they resided in the four corners area, the Aztec Nation developed a civilization covering an area which includes all or portions of the States of Arizona, Utah, Colorado, Oklahoma, Texas, New México, and the Mexican States of Sonora and Chihuahua.

While we do not know for certain when the first Aztec calendar was actually developed, it is very likely that the Aztecs created the calendar before the end of the 1st sun time period or soon thereafter. For certain, the Aztecs were aware of the motions of the sun and of the moon because this knowledge was essential to the creation of the calendar. Also, archaeological evidence [a massive stone wheel] found on the open plains in the State of Wyoming suggests that the designers of the wheel knew about the motions of the sun. This massive stone wheel and its spokes are perfectly aligned with the summer solstice, winter solstice, and the spring and fall equinox.[23]

Could the ancient homeland of the Aztec during the 1st *sol* time have been near the area where this massive stone wheel still

22   This significant historical finding established a written history in the United States for the Aztecs, and for their descendants, the Chicanos, and other Native Americans such as the Hopi, Zuni, Keres, Tewa, Tanoans, Yaqui, Pueblo, Shoshoni, Ute, etc. This historical information makes the Chicanos and these other Native American nations among the oldest, if not the oldest, living Americans in the United States with a recorded history.

23   Williamson, Ray A. *Living the Sky, the Cosmos of the American Indian* (University of Oklahoma Press).

exists today [Bighorn Medicine Wheel, Wyoming]? According to weather historians, that area in Wyoming experienced an ice age around 1400 B.C. According to the history recorded in The Book of the Sun, the Aztecs abandoned their 1st ancient homeland because of the ice age in the year 1386 B. C. Additionally, the ancient northern hunting grounds of the Aztecs could not have been very far north from the Green River Basin in Utah. Aztec history records that they arrived in the four corners area, their 2nd home site, the same year they departed their ancient homeland. Their 1st migration started and ended the same year, 1386 B. C.

After arriving in Utah, the Aztecs developed the first calendar, which continued in use for 52 years. Our current calendar spans only one year. Consequently, we replace our calendar every year. The 3,000 plus year old calendar developed by the Aztecs is more accurate than the one we use today. The Aztec calendar spans 52 years and can be used over again for a subsequent 52 year period. It never ends.

THE SECOND SUN: THE OLD, OLD, COLORFUL LAND

In 1386 B.C., at the end of the 1st sun time period, the Aztecs moved south in search of a warmer climate and for a living environment which would provide better protection from the elements and predators. When they arrived at the four corners area, they built their homes in caves and hollows in the cliffs. Over time, these caves and hollows were enlarged. Some were converted into cliff dwellings that were difficult to access and easy to defend from four-legged predators and two-legged enemies. Somewhat later, they built houses made of stones and adobe. Some of these stone buildings had walls five feet thick that supported apartment buildings four stories high. These structures contained *kivas*,[24] large ceremonial buildings, which could hold up to 500 people at a time.

In his writing, Dr. Rivas-Salmón concluded that the "Rain of Fire" ended in the year 502 B.C. Therefore, the Aztecs resided

24   *Kiva*, a large circular underground chamber usually used for religious ceremonies. These chambers were also used for public gathering, socializing, work, recreation, and prayer.

in the four corners area a total of 884 years. As to what caused the "Rain of Fire" or the "Rain of Heat," Dr. Rivas-Salmón mentioned the heating of the earth's atmosphere causing a great drought as a possible explanation. According to Dr. Rivas-Salmón, this warming of the earth atmosphere caused a heat wave, which did not allow snow to form in the Rocky Mountains.[25]

This cartouche, *Xiu-Quiahuilt-Tonatuih*, *Sol de Lluvia de Fuego*, Sun of Rain of Fire, the 2nd catastrophe which ended the 2nd sol time period and "caused the Aztecs to abandon their homeland in the four corners area and move south seeking the moisture of the tropics."[1] In this pictogram you have the four winds, *tanallo*. The four circles in each corner of the cartouche represent the four winds. The four symbols with a white top, a blue middle and a white bottom between the two winds on the top portion of the cartouche represent the symbol for fire, *xiu*, or heat. In the middle of the cartouche, lays the blue symbol for rain, *quiahuitl*[2]. Therefore, we can read this symbol to mean, "Rain of Fire," or "Rain of Heat."

---

1   Orozco (18).

2   *Quiahuitl,* rain in Nahautl, hundreds of years later still remains with us as an expression, *que ahuite*, meaning what a shame; an expression used whenever someone "rains on your parade."

---

25   Ibid.

Without snow, there was no snowmelt and consequently no headwaters for the four rivers. The rivers dried up, and the Aztec could not irrigate their crops. The Aztecs had no choice but to

Huehuetlapallan, the old, old colorful land includes the Grand Canyon and sites such as Rainbow Bridge in the State of Utah. Several natural land bridges exist throughout the four corners area and these bridges were used as special religious ceremonial locations. Under these bridges, the Aztec would perform their religious offerings to their God(s).

evacuate the four corners area, the land they lovingly referred to as *Huehuetlapallan*, "the old, old, colorful land," and what Chicanos currently refer to as the heart of Aztlán. This area includes several notable geographic areas: Monument Valley, Mesa Verde National Park, the Painted Desert, Rainbow Bridge, Canyon De Chelly National Park, and the Grand Canyon. The heart of Aztlán is indeed an old, old, colorful land!

When visiting the Aztec ruins north of Flagstaff, Arizona, including Oraibi, Shongopovi, Hotevilla, the Petrified Forest National Monument in the Painted Desert area and in Canyon De Chelly National Monument, we noticed several old lava flows. Upon closer examination of the area, we found numerous sites, which contained lava rocks as if these smaller lava rocks had been casted out by eruptions, and a few lava flows as well. We studied a satellite image of this same geographical area, which showed at least eleven volcanic cones just northeast of Flagstaff, near the San Juan Mountains.

At Bandelier National Monument Park, in New México, we observed numerous cliff houses and caves, which were carved out of the lava rock. These cliff dwellings were once the homes of our Aztec ancestors. The lava materials, which were removed to form the dwellings, could have been mixed with water and dry grass to form adobe bricks and walls.

Could the "Rain of Fire" have been volcanic eruptions in the year 502 B.C? Local residents of the four corners area informed us of the existence of numerous volcanic cones in the area. Volcanologists have documented volcanic eruptions in the area around 1000 A. D. Could similar volcanic eruptions have occurred 1,502 years earlier around 502 B. C.? Could those earlier eruptions have been covered over by the more recent lava flows?

Within the Grand Canyon there are several old lava flows from the distant past, which halted the flow of the mighty Colorado River and then altered its course. The geological evidence shows that these lava dams were eventually overcome and worn down by the impressive power and the patience of the mighty Colorado River.

Volcanic eruptions would have caused massive thermo flows plus a "rain of fire" if you will. Hot ash and lava rocks deposited in the four corners area could have melted the snow locally and in the nearby mountains, causing flooding, massive soil erosion,[26] and later, a drought. The "rain of fire" and the extreme heat from the eruptions and the forest fires would have melted all the snow in the area. The ash deposits would have covered their fields, and with no snowmelt to create the headwaters for the four rivers, their lifeline

---

26   Several archaeological studies have documented extensive soil erosion in the four corners area.

to water would have dried up. Several archaeologists who have studied the ruins in the four corners area have documented "massive soil erosion," "flooding," and volcanic pebbles throughout the area. These occurrences would have comprised a great catastrophe for the residents.

THE THIRD SUN: THE LAND OF THE EGRETS

The 3rd Sun, the Sun of Wind, started at the conclusion of the 2nd Sun time period, in the year 502 B.C. Most of the survivors of the "Rain of Fire" catastrophe gathered their belongings, sealed their homes and departed. Historical evidence indicates that some survivors opted to stay; most moved further south. It is estimated that there may have been more than half a million survivors of the "rain of fire." To facilitate migration, the Aztec Nation divided into smaller, more manageable groups. Each group was searching for a new homeland. Some remained in the four corners area. One group migrated south by following the west side of the Rocky Mountains into México where the same mountain range becomes known as Las Sierras Madre, into what is now the States of Sonora and Chihuahua. Other Aztec groups migrate south following the Río Colorado into the Sea of Córtez and then further south along the west coast of the Sea of Córtez. These two groups met and joined forces again at *Culhuacan*, the place where the mountains curve. At this location, the Sierra Madre mountain range turns towards the Sea of Córtez and then turns inland again forming an elbow, and that is why the Aztecs named the location Culhuacan, meaning the place where the mountain turns. Hundreds of years later, the conquering Spaniards had trouble pronouncing the name *Culhuacan*, and changed it to Culiacan, the current capitol of the State of Sinaloa, México.

The Aztecs conquered and then evicted some of the former residents of Culhuacan and the surrounding areas. The Aztecs referred to this new homeland as *Aztlán*, the land of the egrets. *Azta* means egret, and the suffix *tlan*, means the place of; the two terms jointed together become *Aztlán*, the place of the egrets. During their stay in the Culhuacan region (810 years), the Aztecs established sev-

41

en cities in seven different valleys, a city at each entrance (*oztoc*) to each valley. The new homeland became known as *Chicomostoc*. A great civilization flourished once more.

Each valley had a river and farmland which could be irri-

Chicomoztoc, the "Seven Caves," and the beginning of the Mexica migration from their third home-land they called *Aztlán*, as depicted in the Codex Durán, taken from the *Museo Nacional de Antrop-ología*, México, D.F.[1] One of the few reminding codices which were not burn, this codex depicts the Aztecs talking to their families and neighbors in each village before they decided to leave the area, taking with them all their weapons, families and personal belongings, just as *Tonatiuh* had instructed them.

---

1   Carrasco (1992), p.6.

gated, an abundance of birds, deer, and plenty of wild animals. As a result of the abundant flora and fauna in the region, the Aztecs prospered and their population grew. The numerous exotic birds provided plenty of beautiful feathers, which they valued as highly as gold.

Ehecatonatiuh, Sol de Viento, The Wind Sun, the 3rd *sol* time period begins in 502 B.C. and ended in 308 A.D. The figure in the middle of the cartouche with four teeth is the Aztec symbol for *Ehecatl*, their God of Wind, and again, the four circles in the four corners of the cartouche represent the four winds.

During the 810 years, they resided at Chicomostoc; the Aztecs harvested the wealth of the natural resources, farmed, and established trade with other Native Nations. Consequently, their power and influence spread throughout the other civilizations of México.

At Culhuacan, the Aztecs had ball courts identical to the ones found in the Yucatan peninsula. A rubber ball was needed to play this game. It seems reasonable to assume that the Aztecs traded with people who had access to *ule*, rubber, either the Olmecs [27] or

This Mexica codex, known as "Codex Boturini," depicts the Aztec leaving *Aztlán*, their homeland (Note the seven homes.), and departing by boat, down the Pacific coast, taking their home-fire with them in their travel (footsteps). This codex resides in the *Museo Nacional de Antropología*, México, D.F.

the Mayas, or both.

In the year 308 A.D., their Sun God, *Tonatiuh*, once again decided His people must move, and therefore, ordered the great wind, *Ehecatl*, to send severe hurricanes to destroy *Chicomostoc*. The Aztec civilization suffered a mighty devastating blow and was almost destroyed by these hurricanes.

It was indeed a major catastrophe, and once again the Aztec survivors obeyed their Sun God and abandoned their homeland in the State of Sinaloa and moved further south.

Some Mexica moved south and inland on foot, toward the Valley of Anahuac. Most of the Aztecs moved south alone the Pacific coast, some by land, and others by boat. They settled in the land of the deer, in the community of Mazatlán (*mazatl*, deer, *tlan*,

27   The term Olmec derides from the Nahuatl terms *ule*, meaning rubber, and *mecas* meaning workers; as such, Ulmecas in the Nahuatl language (rubberworkers) became Olmecas in Spanish, and Olmecs in English.

Nahui Tonatiuh, the 4th Sun time period was call the *Atl Tonatiuh*, the Sun of Water. Severe rain storms caused massive flooding and inundation of their community in the year 1116 A.D. causing the Aztecs to abandon their homes and once again moved in search of a new home site.

the place of), in the State of Sinaloa, México.

THE FOURTH SUN: IN THE LAND OF DEER

In 308 A.D., the Aztec began the 4th sol, the Nahui Tonatiuh, on the coast of the *Oceano Pacífico*[28] (Peaceful Ocean) in the community of Mazatlán. Once again they prospered and developed a thriving community based on agriculture, hunting and fishing. They probably also reverted to their former practices of commerce, agriculture, and trading with their neighbors.

In the year 308 A.D., the Aztecs arrived at the Mazatlán area and established an empire, which lasted until 1116 A.D. (808 years). Then, once again, according to their history, the Aztec God destroyed their community for the fourth time. The Aztec believed

---

28   In 1523, Hernan Cortez, led by Native guides, became the first European to see this ocean for the first time. He was so amazed by the clam soothing waves that washed onto the beach that he named the body of water, *El Mar Pacífico*, The Peaceful Ocean.

that *Tonatiuh* was angry with them and had intentionally sent severe rainstorms to cause inundations. So once again, His children, the Aztecs, were forced to abandon their homes.

An artist rendition of what the temples at Tenochtitlán look like in 1519. Rendition was copied from the *Museo de Historia y Antropología* de México.

THE FIFTH SUN: TENOCHTITLAN

This time, as a punishment, the Aztecs would wander throughout central México searching for a homeland for 209 years (about ten generations). They hired themselves out as mercenaries for other local Native nations. In exchange for these services they receive subsistence and temporary home sites. In the tenth generation of wandering, they were finally given permission to inhabit a small, snake infested inland, in the middle of Lake Texcoco.

Aztec legend states that *Tonatiuh* had instructed them to search for a home wherever they found an eagle perched on a cactus devouring a snake. And according to legend, they found such a place in the year 1325 A.D. on an island. The island had no fresh, clean drinking water. For months, they hauled their drinking water in jars, by boat. Shortly thereafter, they constructed a stone and mortar aqueduct to transport fresh water from a spring on the main land, over the lake and onto their island.

46

Almost 200 years later, by 1519, according to the conquering Spaniards, *Tenochtitlán* was probably the largest population center in the world, and certainly the largest city in North America and probably in South America as well. It was indeed a beautiful city.

This artistic rendition of *El Templo Mayor* (Main Temple) was copied from the *Museo de Historia y Antropología* de México.

One can only wonder at the immense labor involved in transporting all the building materials for the temples, the homes, and the buildings onto the island. All the building materials came from places miles away and transported across Lake Texcoco by boats or rafts. A monumental task, when one considers the size of the buildings, the huge temples, the thousands of homes, and the size of public plazas paved with stone.

This once snake-infested island became the beautiful City of Tenochtitlán, with a population of well over a quarter of a million people, with canals, streets, plazas, market places, religious temples, and a sewage system. Every home had fresh drinking water and an indoor toilet, which was automatically flushed every third day. The City of *Tenochtitlán* had one aqueduct with two waterways. According to Dr. Rivas-Salmón, one waterway was in use while the other was being cleaned. Upon completion of the cleaning, the waterway was flushed and so were the toilets.

Chapter II: *El Segundo Sol*, the Second Sun

According to the history recorded in the "Aztec Calendar," the 1st epoch ended in the year 1386 B.C., the same year the Aztecs departed from their hunting grounds when their northern homeland became covered with deep snow and then ice. They migrated southward settling in the four corners area of the southwestern United States over 3,396 [as of 2010] years ago.[29] These ancient Americans came from some northern location, probably Canada, or the current states of Wyoming or Montana, and settled in the Green River basin in southern Utah. The oldest archaeological findings in the four corners area have been uncovered here.

Documented in the "Aztec Calendar" is the 2nd sun time period, which lasted from 1386 B.C. to 502 B. C., at least 884 years. During this period, the Aztecs established the largest agriculture-based civilization in the American Southwest and probably in the North American continent.

Dr. Orozco and Dr. Rivas-Salmón stated that the Aztec settlement of the four corners area in the year 1386 B. C. is recorded in the Book of the Sun, also known as "the Aztec Calendar." According to the documented history in this historic relic, the Aztecs settled and lived in the four corners area for 884 years. During their stay in the American Southwest, these Native Americans developed a civilization based primarily on agriculture and supplemented by hunting, gathering, and trade. Based on what they accomplished, we can consider their civilization one of the most advanced in the North American continent. This ancient homeland of the Aztecs, from 1386 B.C. to 502 B.C., became the geographical area currently known as the States of Arizona, Utah, Colorado, New México, parts of Oklahoma parts of Texas, and the Mexican states of Chihuahua and Sonora.

This new homeland of the Aztecs afforded warmer climate, better protection from the elements, predators, enemies, and access to game animals. They set up shelters in caves and cliff crevices,

29   This significant historical finding established a written history in the United States for the Aztecs, and for their descendants, the Mexican American, or Chicanos as some of them prefer to be called. This historical information makes the Chicanos one of the oldest groups of living Americans in the United States with a recorded history, over three thousand (3,000+) years.

sites which were easy to defend and difficult to access. With time, some of these shelters were converted into larger living spaces. Individual rooms were carved into the crevices. The dwellings were enlarged and extended by removing material from the face of the cliffs.

The waste material was mixed with water and dry grass and formed into building blocks we now call *adobes*. These building blocks were used to further fortify the entrances to the cliff dwellings and to the caves.

Over time, as the population grew and the building projects increased, the homes became formidable and impressive cliff dwellings. Some of these residential sites were difficult to find, most were challenging to access, and all were easy to defend from four-legged predators and two-legged enemies. These shelters, built in secluded crevices and caves facing southwest, provided maximum exposure to the warm sun in winter.

Initially, all these homes were one story. As the population grew and more space was needed for homes and storage, a second and then a third story were added. Timbers were needed to sustain the 2nd and 3rd story rooms. This multi-story construction within the cliff dwellings may have been added hundreds of years after the initial settlement in the crevices and caves.

As the new Aztec homeland became more secure and as the population grew, the Aztecs built stone houses on open ground. Wood beams were required to support the ceilings. On the ground, some of these stone buildings had five-foot thick walls that supported four-story high structures. Some of these structures included *kivas*[30], large enclosed public social and ceremonial centers, which could accommodate up to 500 people at a time.

Other accomplishments included public roads, cliff dwellings, cities, ball courts, *kivas* (public places), dams, irrigation ca-

30   *Kiva*, a large circular underground chamber usually used for religious ceremonies. These chambers were also used for public gathering, work, play, and prayer.

nals, and numerous farming villages. Other structures included: a convention center and a university at Pueblo Bonito, New México; an astronomical observation post in Casa Grande, Arizona; a very large ball court in Snake Town, Arizona; and numerous smaller ball courts throughout the area.

Roads extending hundreds of miles connected their population centers and facilitated trade. The roads were as straight as an arrow and 30 feet wide. These roads started in Utah, extended into southern Colorado, down into New México, across into Casa Grande, Arizona, and then north again into Utah. One of these roads extended from Mesa Verde National Park in the State of Colorado well into the communities of *Casas Grandes* (Big Houses) in the Mexican State of Chihuahua, and into the community of Trincheras, Sonora, México.

These major roads facilitated trade and travel within their extended communities connecting their villages and the numerous agricultural fields, which were hundreds of miles apart. The roads also provided access to other Native tribes living outside their area.

When the Aztecs migrated from the four corners area they left behind a legacy of artifacts and cliff dwellings, which are found in numerous locations, including: Mesa Verde National Park, Chaco Canyon, Canyon De Chelly, in canyons along the Colorado River, Green River, Little Colorado River, Gila River, Salt River, and the San Juan River. The Aztecs constructed a few large communities that in modern times have become major tourist attractions, such as Casa Grande, Arizona; Pueblo Bonito, New México; and Mesa Verde National Park. Numerous other similar building sites in and around the four corners area have been uncovered and partially restored. Many of these archaeological sites are still in ruins, but some structures are still standing today. Some restored sites, such as Mesa Verde National Park, have become major tourist attractions and sources of income for local residents.

More Aztec sites are still being uncovered in the four corners

As an example of the beautiful dwelling the Aztecs left behind, we offer this "Cliff Palace." In 1888, this magnificent city was re-discovered by Richard Wetherill and Charlie Mason, two cowboys from Colorado, who named it "Cliff Palace." It is located near the city of Córtez, Colorado, where it has become the "crown jewel" of Mesa Verde National Park. The dwelling stands about 6,790 feet above sea level, is twenty-five feet high, extends 324 feet long – roughly 80 feet longer than the Great Sphinx at Giza, and probably housed more than 400 people. To reach this magnificent site, a person has to descend a 100-foot steep trail and then climb up five eight-foot ladders. Because the site is difficult to access, it was perfect for defense purposes.

area even today. Among the most beautiful restored cliff dwellings are the ones in Mesa Verde National Park in Colorado.

The stone building and cliff dwellings in Aztec Ruins National Park, near the community of Aztec, New México, are the only ruins in the four corners area named after the builders. Research by Dr. Orozco and Dr. Rivas-Salmón documents that these ruins are Aztec. *The Book of the Sun* further supports the assertion that these ancient ruins, especially the cliff dwellings, were built by the Aztecs.

The American Southwest had been settled and domesticated with numerous villages, towns, and extensive irrigated farmlands flowering at the time that Europe was still experiencing the Dark

Ages. Archaeological evidence found in these ruins strongly indicates that the claim by American writers of history that white men explored, settled, and "tamed the wild west" in reality is just a myth, a creation perpetuated by biased historians of European ancestry, fiction writers and Hollywood movies.

These myth demeanishes the amazing accomplishment of these Native Americans. The numerous towns they constructed of stone, the multiple-unit housing structures, five-story high buildings, public roads, public buildings, and convention centers all bear testimony to the subtleties and complexities of this ancient civilization. These true pioneers and settlers of the "wild west" were hunting, gathering, farming in the river bottoms, and building cities in the four corners area at least 2,878 years before Columbus landed on an island off the North American continent.

They constructed vast water reservoirs and dug canals to divert rainwater and rivers into irrigation ditches, which watered thousands of acres of farmland in the American Southwest. Farming provided a stable and dependable source of food, which allowed the Aztecs to develop an advanced civilization with a structured division of labor. These accomplishments in turn facilitated public building projects such as roads, communal living areas, and even public facilities for recreation and socializing as well.

The first American archaeologists who excavated these sites labeled these ruins "*Anasazi* Ruins" because they were ignorant of the history of the Aztecs in the United States. They claimed that an ancient American Native tribe or tribes, which they could not identify, built the cliff dwellings and the numerous farming villages they uncovered. American archaeologists employed Navajo workers in Colorado and Utah to research out and excavate ancient archaeological sites. The Navajo workers referred to these sites as belonging to "*anasazi*," meaning "ancient enemies." Consequently, the archaeologists, thereafter, referred to these sites as the ruins of the "*Anazasi*" with full knowledge that no such Native Nation had ever existed in the United States.

In Arizona, along the Gila River the archaeologists were employing Pima guides and workers. The Pimas referred to these ancient Aztec sites as the ruins belonging to the "*Hohokam.*" In modern Pima language Hohokam means "those that have departed." The archaeologists were satisfied with crediting the fictional "*Hohokam*" with the establishment of an agricultural civilization, which was without equal, rather than taking the effort to identify the actual builders, the ancient Aztecs.

The archaeologists were confronted with evidence of a civilization able to construct highly advanced agriculture systems comprised of canals, which were more than 50 feet wide, feeding smaller canals and hundreds of smaller irrigation ditches irrigating at least 100,000 acres of farmland in the communities around Casa Grande and Snake Town, Arizona. They assigned credit to a tribe, the "*Hohokam,*" named by their workers, although no such Native Nation ever existed in the American Southwest.

In northern Arizona, an American archaeologist named the sites in that area as "the ruins of the 'Sinagua' Indians." "*Sin agua*" means "without water" in Spanish. In the 16th century, Spaniards seeking to conquer the local Natives, surrounded a group living in these sites. The Spaniards tried to force the Natives out of their barricaded homes by cutting their water supply. They stationed soldiers around a creek believing they had secured the only source of water. A few months later the Spaniards gave up and thereafter referred to these Natives as "*Indios sin agua,*" meaning "Indians without water."

Hundreds of years later an American archaeologist excavating the ancient sites in the area and referred to these archaeological ruins as the "ruins of the "Sinagua" Indians. The archaeologist failed to research that no such Native Nation was ever named *sinagua*. He may have felt that to the unsuspecting English language reader, "Sinagua" sounded like an Native Nation name, as do the terms: *Anazasi*, Salados, *Mogollon*, *Chacoans*, Mesa Verdeans and Hohokam. The mislabeling continued at an ancient Aztec site near

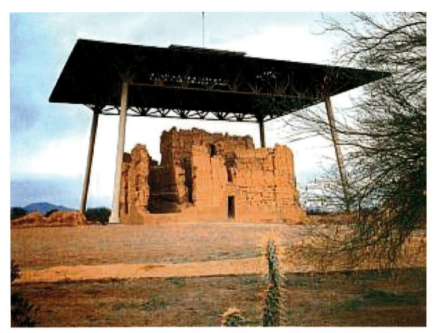

Casa Grande ruins, picture taken by Wyman Sanders. This is one of the main buildings still standing today in the community of Casa Grande, Arizona. Some believe this building was five stories high, and probably used as an astrological observatory. The Aztecs were keen observers of the sky, the cosmos, and the universe.

Río Salado (Salted River) Arizona, known today as Salt River. The ancient Aztec inhabitants who had built their homes there were mislabeled *Salados* (Salted) Indians. The archaeologists assumed that these Salados were descendants of the Hohokam. According to David Grant Noble, "an authority" on ancient ruins of the southwest, "*Salado* culture is considered to be a blend of native and local traditions with influences from the *Hohokam* and Pueblo cultures."[31]

Along the Little Colorado River, archaeologists found ancient ruins of a Native civilization they opted to name the *Mogollon*, because the local mountain range in the area is named the Mogollon Mountains. The mountains were named from a seventeenth-century governor of the *Provincia de Nuevo México*. The *Mogollon* Natives supposedly settled the area of Northern Arizona and Northwest New México and the Casa Grande, Arizona, area as well. According to the archaeologists, these Natives probably became the ancestors of

31   Noble, David Grant. 2000, *Ancient Ruins of the Southwest*, Northland Publishing Company (Flagstaff,

the *Salados* and *Sinaguas*.

In northern New México the Aztecs are called "Chacoans" because their ruins were found in Chaco Canyon. In the State of Utah, they became the "Fremont Indians" because their ruins were found near the Fremont River. In southern Colorado, the Aztec became the "Mesa Verdeans" because these Natives lived in the Mesa Verde area. It is almost like calling some of our citizens, "New Yorkers," "Texans," "Californians," "New Mexicans," "Yankees," "Rebels," "Iowans," etc., without mentioning the fact that they are all Americans. The individual(s) who set these fictional labels may have found it difficult to believe that mere "Indians" could have established such a magnificent civilization as the one created by the ancient Aztecs.

As to the Navajo term anazasi, the Aztecs, more than likely, were the ancient enemies of the Navajo and of several other Native tribes in the immediate area as well. The Aztecs have a long history of evicting or conquering Native tribes in their immediate area and then forcing them to pay tribute (taxes). According to their enemies, the Aztecs were ferocious and fearless warriors. However, "Aztec wars did not have conquest as their primary goal; neither did they – except in most unusual cases – seek the enemy's annihilation. Their aim was to subjugate the enemy and force them to pay tribute. The idea of empire, in the sense of a pluri-national society in which one state governs and dominates all others, never appeared at any time in Meso-America – not even in the expansionist periods of Tula and Tenochtitlán."[32]

As to the term "*hohokam*," meaning "those that have departed," in the Pima language, this term certainly was not the name of the human beings who lived in the deserts of Arizona at that time. The Aztecs established numerous villages, farming communities, and cities within Arizona, especially along the Gila, Colorado and the Little Colorado Rivers. Among their largest communities was Casa Grande, Arizona, which had an astrological observation post

---

32   Octavio Paz, "Will for Form," *México, Splendors of Thirty Centuries*, p. 11.

and hundreds of acres of farmland irrigated by a canal system, which provided running water all year long.

When most of the Aztecs departed the area in 502 B.C., some Aztecs remained behind and years later became known as the Pimas. Some historians believe that the *Pima*, as well as several other Native tribes in the American Southwest, are probably descendants of the Aztec Nation that created this vast and extraordinary Native American civilization in the American Southwest. We believe some Aztecs and their descendants, those that remained in the area, hundreds of years later, became known by other names such as Hopi, Zuni, Pueblo, Pima, Yaqui, Ute, Piute, Shoshone, Comanche, and other lesser known Native tribes. Some of these descendants remained in the area and their descendants later re-occupied the abandoned cliff dwellings and stone buildings—the homes left behind by the "ancient enemies" of the Navajo and "those who departed."

Almost a thousand years later, in 1540, the Spaniard explorer Francisco Vásquez de Coronado and other Spanish explorers that followed him, re-named these human beings, the *Salados* (Salted) Indians and the "*Indios sin agua*" (Indians without water), and the "Pueblo" (Town) Natives because the latter Native Americans lived in small *pueblos* (towns). More than five hundred years later American archaeologists continued the renaming of these Aztec ruins by fictitious names such as *Anasazi, Mogollon, Hohokam, Chacoans, Mesa Verdeans, Fremont, Sinagua, Salados*, etc.

In an area currently known as Snake Town, Arizona, a small, deserted area located between the communities of Phoenix and Tucson, an archaeologist uncovered 29 huge mounds of garbage. Also uncovered were a very large ancient farming community, building sites containing hundreds of living areas, and a large Maya-type ball court. The ball court had been dug into the landscape and was partially submerged below ground level. Because this ball court was submerged and identical in size to the Maya's ball courts in the Yucatan peninsula, the archaeologist suspected that at one time in the distant past, this ball court probably was surrounded by walls with viewing areas as well. Also, because a rubber ball was needed to play this game, the residents must have established trade with other Native Nations reaching well into the Southern Gulf Coast of México, where *ule*, rubber, is produced from trees.

In this same area, several water canals and large irrigational ditches were uncovered. Apparently, these ancient farmers were irrigating and farming thousands of acres in the Arizona desert hundreds of years before Columbus' grandparents were born. This magnificent civilization built living quarters four and five stories tall, ball courts, kivas, public roads, and market places. They established trade, cared for their elderly, and raised their families in "The Wild West" thousands of years before Europeans knew this advanced civilization existed.

Taking all these accomplishments by ttNative civilizations into account, I find it hard to believe the American myth of the "Indian Savages." Did the white settlers who migrated across North America have to conquer, civilize, or exterminate the "Red Man" as Benjamin Franklin advocated: "Complete extirpation of the Indians?" Did the "Wild West" perpetuated by literature, newspapers, and later Hollywood exist outside the communities of white Europeans made up of outlaws and individuals unconstrained by a system of laws and order? Could it have been the white Europeans who were the savages, the cruel, uncivilized, and inferior human beings that appropriated the hunting grounds of the Native Americans (whose ancestors occupied the land for thousands of years.) so that the land could be sold, cultivated and its natural resources harvested?

The ancient residents of Snake Town, Arizona, conducted the Aztec ritual of destroying their old possessions at the end of each 52 years cycle. They performed this religious ceremony 29 times before they departed the area. American archaeologists uncovered 29 large mounds of garbage in this area. These 29 huge piles of garbage attracted mice and rats. The rodents attracted snakes, hence the name of the area, Snake Town.

The 29 mounds of garbage, to an archaeologist, translate into archaeological treasures, which they dig, gather, clean, and then study while being careful not to bother the snakes. To students of the Aztec civilization, these garbage mounds translate into historical events. These mounds of garbage indicate that these ancient residents lived approximately 1,508 years (29 X 52 calendar years) in that area before they departed. If these Aztecs according to the "Aztec Calendar" arrived at this location around 1386 B.C. and if they departed approximately 1,508 years later, the year of departure according to the math was around 122 A.D[33]. These ancient communities in Southern Arizona may lay a sufficient distance from the volcanic eruptions that occurred in the San Juan Mountains in the north in 502 B.C. so that the "rain of fire" may not have reached them. Possibly their farmlands in this area were not completely destroyed. Consequently, these Aztecs residing in the communities surrounding Snake Town, Arizona, probably remained in the area after their brothers living further north departed in 502 B.C.

More than a thousand years later, in 1540 A.D., when the Spanish explorer, Francisco Vásquez de Coronado,[34] became the first European to explore that area, he stumbled into these ancient Aztec ruins. He was amazed at the size of a building that he found among the ruins, and therefore, named the site *Casa Grande*, meaning "Big House." He was referring to the large building (page 55), which we are currently trying to preserve. American archaeologists believe this building may have been used as an astronomical observation post. The Aztecs were avid students of the night skies, the movement of the sun, the moon, the stars, and the planets.

As an example of how the Aztecs studied the skies, and possibly arrived at 365 days a year calendar, they observed that the Morning Star appears in the east. It is the first star seen just before

33   During our field research we found only one town, Vicom, Sonora, México, with a museum and a plaque which stated: "In 552 A.D., the Yoeme [Yaqui] Tribe broke off the Toltec Nation and chose to remain behind." The Toltec Nation moved south, into the Valley of Anahuac.

34   Our American History books refer to this Spanish explorer as Francisco V. Coronado. In the Spanish language, his correct name is Francisco Vásquez de Coronado; Vásquez being his father's surname and Coronado being his mother's surname. If we do not want to continue the Spanish tradition of including the mother's surname, then our American History books should refer to this Spanish explorer as Francisco C. Vásquez, not as we erroneously do today, Francisco V. Coronado.

the sun comes up every day for 236 consecutive days. Then, it disappears for 348 days before it re-appears again, a cycle of 584 days. They also observed that the Evening Star appears in the west, usually the first star seen in the early evening. It is usually the first star seen at sunset and becomes the largest, brightest star in the west. It appears for 250 consecutive days. Then it disappears for 334 days before it appears again, a total of 584 days. They suspected that the Morning and Evening Stars might be the same star; each had a complete cycle, which took 584 days. They studied the Morning Star and the Evening Stars as one cycle. The Morning Star would appear in the east for 236 days, then it disappeared for 90 days, and then on the 91st day the Evening Star would appear in the west for 250 days and disappear for 8 days (a total of 584 days). On the following day the Morning Star would reappear in the east and thus a new cycle would begin. They realized that the Evening Star and Morning Star were the same star. Now we know that it is not a start, but a planet named Venus.

Within a couple of decades, they discovered that by taking one complete cycle of the planet Venus (584 days) and multiplying it by 5 and then dividing the total by 8, they got 365 days, one complete calendar year. According to Dr. Rivas-Salmón, this process is how the Aztec arrived at the 365 days calendar year. We can also hypothesize that they might have also discovered the 365 days cycle by simple observation of the position of the sun, noting that after 365 days the sun would return back to the exact same position. Years later, they discovered that every four years, they needed to add a day to the fourth year (366 days – leap year) and that is when they developed the 52-year calendar.

This 52-year calendar is reflected in the Book of the Sun. For example, the Morning Star is the light colored face of *Quetzalcoatl* (the plumed serpent) at the bottom of the Book of the Sun; the Evening Star is the darker colored face of *Quetzalcoatl*. *Quetzalcoatl's* body has 13 sections and 4 rattles (the white ribbons). If one multiplies 13 by 4 we get 52, the number of years in an Aztec

Calendar.[35] Therefore, the Aztec calendar ended on the 13th leap year; thus one of the reasons why in the Aztec culture the number 13 was considered a very lucky number.

The archaeological site of the *"Sinagua"* had an aquifer the inhabitants used as a water supply. The Spaniards did not know about this water source and at the time thought the local Natives could live without water; therefore, they identified them as *"Indios sin agua,"* "Indians without water." To identify any group of people by such terms as *"Sinagua," "Anazasi," "Salado," "Fremonts," "Mogollon," "Chacoans," "Mesa Veredeans,"* or *"Hohokam"* is inaccurate.

The Aztecs were most likely the "ancient enemies of the Navajos," and they were also the American Natives "who departed" from their homeland in 502 B.C. and in 122 A.D They were Aztec or as other Native Nations referred to them, Mejicas, or Meshica, meaning people of the sun. The Navajos, the Hopi, and the Pueblo Natives have voiced their dislike of terms like "anazasi," "hohokam," and "sinagua," which they find insulting.

Based on the recorded history contained in *El Libro del Sol*, the Aztecs were the American Natives who lived in the four corners area of the United States since 1386 B.C.; the same geographical area that current Mexican American citizens and Chicanos call the heart of *Aztlán*. According to Dr. Orozco, the term *Aztlán* in the Nahuatl language means the "land of the egrets." Today, Chicanos use this term, *Aztlán*, to identify the Aztecs' ancient homeland in the American Southwest.

Cliff dwellings and other stone buildings are still standing today. The reservoirs, canals, and irrigation ditches the Aztecs built to irrigate their crops are still in evidence today. Some new sites are being discovered, preserved, excavated, and a few are being restored and studied.

---

35   Re-visit the "Aztec Calendar" on page 24 to observe the 13 sections, the color of the faces, rattles, etc.

Cuauhtémoc, *La Aguila Que Descende del Cielo*, Descending Eagle from the Sky, the last Aztec Emperor [1520-21], from a painting by the famous Mexican artist, Jesús Enrique Emilio de la Helguera Espinoza. He produced this work for the *Cigarrera La Moderna, S. A. de C.V.* that used this painting for promoting cigarettes. The painting appeared in numerous calendars in México in the 1940s, 1950s, and 1960s. The Aztecs had two elite warrior orders that any young man could try to join, the Order of the Jaguar and the Order of the Eagle. In this painting by de la Helguera Espinosa, Cuauhtémoc is wearing the attire of an Eagle Warrior.

These cities, villages, and cliff dwellings, contain buildings, which were four and five stories high, with ball courts, conference centers, market places, religious centers and other structures. Some of these ruins are partially standing today. Other archaeological sites are so old that only the foundations remain. Precious artifacts have been and are still being snatched by "visitors" who plunder these archaeological sites. These priceless artifacts are irreplaceable and extremely important to the understanding of the complete history and heritage of the Aztecs.

The Aztecs believed that their God would end their world at the end of a 52-year cycle. Therefore, they believed that if their God did not end their world on the last day of the 52-year cycle, the world would continue for another 52 years. Consequently, at the

The building on the left is an Aztec ruin in Chaco Canyon, New México, not a cliff dwelling, constructed of stone, housed hundreds of people, and some of the buildings were at least four stories high. On the right, only the foundation remains; one of numerous such buildings. The following photos represent examples of ruins located in the four corners area.

end of the 52-year cycle, they stacked all their old calendars and belongings including pottery, clothing, weapons, blankets, etc. in a great pile and intentionally destroyed all of it. On the first day of the new 52-year cycle, they would have a feast to celebrate God's gift of a new 52-year cycle.

More than two thousand years later, these great piles of garbage are what American archeologists have uncovered in their diggings from the 1890's through today. Several archaeologists have commented in their publications that "some of the items in the garbage piles appeared to have been intentionally destroyed." They were intentionally destroyed [36] as part of the religious ceremony for celebrating the end of a fifty-two year cycle and beginning of a new cycle with a new calendar and new possessions as well.

We believe the *Ute, Shoshoni, Zuñi, Pima, Piute, Hopi, Yaqui, Comanche,* and *Pueblo*, as well as other American Native nations in the American Southwest are direct descendents of the Aztecs who chose to remain in their ancient homeland. We know that some Aztecs opted to remain in the area because they knew the land could sustain a smaller population but not the large population that comprised the Aztec Nation.

Some historians claim that in the *Hopi* language *Anazasi* means "the time-keepers." Either way, the "time-keepers" more than likely refers to the Aztecs who had developed a calendar for keeping track of time, and *"Anazasi,"* meaning the ancient enemies of the *Navajo*, would also identify the Aztecs.

This is another example of an ancient stone building in the four corners area.

36   *National Geographic*, May, 1967, "The Hohokam, First Masters of the American Desert," by Emil W. Haury; National Geographic, Feb. 1964, "Solving the Riddles of Wetherill Mesa," by Douglas Osborne.

The following Aztec ruins are located in the State of Colorado, and in Chaco Canyon, New México. All are located in the four corners area of the American Southwest, the ancient home sites of the Aztecs. These ruins are an example of the beautiful ruins constructed by the Aztecs between 1386 B.C. and 502 B.C. During this time period they not only established and developed a civilization in the American Southwest without equal, they also constructed numerous such beautiful building sites throughout the four corners area, very similar to these ruins. Some ruins are still standing today, but too little is being done to preserve these national treasures.

According to Dr. Rivas-Salmón from the *Universidad Autónoma de Guadalajara,* in 1964, in the four corners area, an American archaeologist, who unearthed sixteen of the huge mounds, published his finding in *National Geographic.* Dr. Rivas-Salmón had read about other American archaeologists who discovered similar artifacts and ruins in and around the four corners area. These archaeologists assigned fictitious names to these discoveries claiming they did not know that they were the artifacts of the Aztec Nation.

In 1971, in Guadalajara, Jalisco, México, I met Dr. Alfonso Rivas-Salmón, a law professor at the *Universidad Autónoma de Guadalajara.* At the time, I was on a special assignment for San Jose State University (SJSU) to explore the possibility of establishing a Spanish Language summer program for graduate students working on a master's degree in the School of Social Work at SJSU. Upon completion of my assignment I met privately with Dr. Rivas-Salmón because I wanted to learn more about the Aztec calendar; at the time, I knew he was one of the world's leading authorities on the history of the Aztecs.

In 1971, on a warm December morning at the Universidad Autónoma de Guadalajara, Jalisco, México, Dr. Rivas-Salmón and I had a scheduled one-hour meeting, which lasted more than five hours. We discussed his findings and his interpretation of the Libro del Sol. He shared with me the story of an article he had read in the February issue of National Geographic in 1964. Dr. Rivas-Salmón told me of an American anthropologist from Boston University, digging in the four corners area, had uncovered ancient American Native ruins and numerous artifacts. Among the archaeologist's findings were 16 huge piles of garbage, as recorded in the article. According to Dr. Rivas-Salmón, in 1967, he wrote the anthropologist a letter asking if he was sure that there were only 16 piles of garbage instead of 17. He did not get an answer to his question that year. During the summer of 1968, the American anthropologist, who was featured in the National Geographic article, made a special trip to Guadalajara to meet with Dr. Rivas-Salmón. The American anthropologist was curious as to how Dr. Rivas-Salmón knew about the 17th mound of garbage. The anthropologist continued digging and searching in the same geographical area the following summer and to his amazement uncovered the 17th mound. Subsequently he retrieved to Dr. Rivas-Salmón' letter, which he had not bothered to answer.

The American anthropologist wondered how Dr. Rivas-Salmón knew so much regarding his discoveries in the four corners area. He wanted to know how Dr. Rivas-Salmón had knowledge of the 17th mound.

One more cliff dwelling, in the four corners area which is difficult to spot, and we found extremely difficult to access.

Dr. Rivas-Salmón, through an English language interpreter, explained to the American archaeologist that he had deciphered the history of the Aztecs as written in El Libro del Sol (the Book of the Sun), and according to the recorded history of the Aztecs, they had lived in the four corners area at least 17 Aztec calendars or 884 years. Dr. Rivas-Salmón knew that if his deciphering of the Book of the Sun was correct, there had to be 17 piles of garbage somewhere in the immediate location within the four corners area. Dr. Rivas-Salmón explained to the American anthropologist that the Aztecs caused the 17 mounds of garbage he uncovered intentionally. Satisfied with Dr. Rivas-Salmón's explanation, the anthropologist from Boston University returned to the United States and continued his excavations.

To our knowledge, this American archaeologist did not correct his writings to reflect that the Aztecs were the ancient people responsible for the artifacts and the ruins. Dr. Rivas-Salmón had proven to him that they were Aztec ruins. However, this American archaeologist, as well other archaeologists, continue to label these findings as the ruins of an ancient Native civilization of unknown origin.

This archaeologists continued to use the previous explanation, "these ruins were so old that we do not know which Indians created them." American Archaeologists continued labeling these ruins "the ruins of the Anazasi," meaning the ancient enemies of the Navajos, even when Dr.Rivas-Salmón had provided documented information that these ruins were Aztec.

The Aztec artifacts found in the four corners area of the American Southwest should have been sufficient evidence to indicate that these archeological sites are Aztec. Additionally, modern day linguists have documented that the languages spoken by American Native tribes who formerly or currently reside in the same geographical area, especially the Utes, Shoshone, Pueblo, Hopi, Pima, Zuñi, Piute, Comanche, and Yaqui have a very strong *Nahuatl* language influence. Linguists call this family of languages spoken by these tribes *Uto-Nahua* or *Uto-Aztecan*.

At one time, in the distant past, possibly as long as 3,396 years ago, these tribes were exposed to the *Nahuatl* language, or they may have been members of the Aztec Nation that spoke Nahuatl. It is possible that in the distant past several of these Native tribes were members of the Aztec Nation before they broke off to seek new lands to settle, to farm, and for new hunting grounds. This process is similar to the migration of the English language, which occurred when the English colonized Canada, the United States, Australia, India, South Africa, and other countries that still speak the English language, although with a variety of accents, inflections and vocabulary.

Roman soldiers, subjects of the Roman Empire, provide another example. Today, the Italian, Portuguese, Spanish, French, and even the English language have a strong Latin influence, which was introduced to these countries by the conquering Romans. The Romans occupied these countries, except for Italy, for approximately four hundred years. The Aztecs resided in the four corners area a minimum of 884 years. They had at least twice as many years as the Roman soldiers to influence the local language(s), and according to modern day linguists, they certainly did.

Before coming to the four corners area, the Aztecs were primarily hunters. In the four corners area, the Aztecs relied heavily on farming, often using irrigation in the river bottoms to grow crops. A calendar or a means for keeping track of time was essential for a farming community. Consequently, to farm, the Aztecs needed to know when to prepare the soil, when to plant, when to harvest, and to keep track of animal migrations, breeding cycles, and rainy seasons.

Archaeological evidence indicates the Aztecs relied on yearly crops of corn, beans, squash, chili, and other edible plants such as wild lettuce, pokeberry, ground berry, Jerusalem artichoke, wolfberries, pecan nuts, piñón nuts, tomatoes, potatoes, and cactus. Some of these berries were dried and eaten during the winter. The Aztecs supplemented their diet with turkey, wild game, snakes, lizards, insects, honey, and fish. They captured wild fowl and gathered roots and edible vegetation.

There is evidence that the Aztecs established trade with other tribes. Archaeologists found no trace of cotton plants in the area, yet they found cotton textiles in the ruins. They also found parrot feathers, California seashells, and other items, not native to the four corners area.[37] The ball courts found in Arizona required a ball made from *ule*, rubber from trees growing in the Mexican Gulf Coast in the Yucatán Peninsula.

When visiting the Aztec ruins north of Flagstaff, Arizona, such as Oraibi, Shongopovi, Hotevilla, the Petrified Forest National Monument, in the Painted Desert area and in Canyon De Chelly, National Monument area, we noticed several old lava flows. Upon closer examination we noticed that the cliff dwellings were constructed of lava rock. This suggested that in the distant, past volcanic eruptions had occurred in that area. Consequently, we decided to study satellite images of this geographical region, which showed eleven volcanic cones in the area, just northeast of Flagstaff, near the San Juan Mountains.[38] We believe that the "Rain of Fire" was volcanic eruptions that occurred in 502 B.C. Volcanologists documented the latest volcanic eruptions in the area in the year 1000 A.D. Evidence such as old lava rocks found in cliff dwellings indicated that there have been earlier eruptions, maybe one around 1,502 years earlier.

Volcanic eruptions can cause massive thermo flows, a "rain of fire" if you will, which burned the wooden structures supporting the massive stone buildings. Hot ash deposits melted the snow in the nearby mountains, causing flooding, massive soil erosion, destroying the farmlands, and days later, the beginnings of a drought. The "rain of fire," the extreme heat from the eruptions, and the forest fires melted all the snow in the area and caused a flood. The ash deposits did cover the farm fields, and without snowmelt to create the headwaters for the rivers, the Aztecs' lifeline to water dried up. Therefore, in 502 B.C., the "Rain of Fire" caused a great natural catastrophe, forcing the ancient civilization to migrate south.

Evidence shows that the Aztec survivors did not leave the

---

37   Some of the information on foods, vegetables, roots, animals, and plants was obtain from archaeological finds documented in an article entitled "Solving the Riddles of Wetherill Mesa," *National Geographic* Magazine, February 1964,

38   We in this paragraph refers to Wyman Sanders and the author.

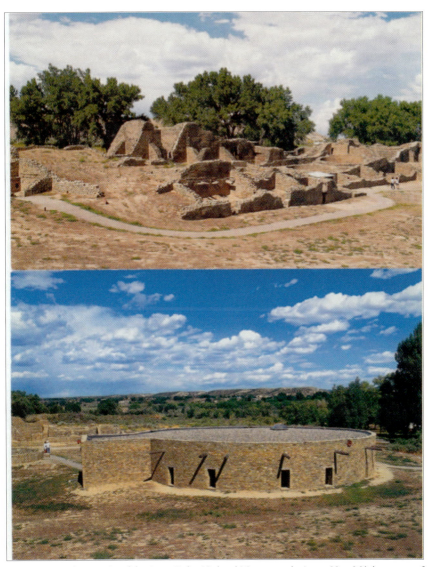

These are two photographs of the Aztec Ruins National Monument, in Aztec, New México, some of the best-preserved ruins in the country. Note the size of the stone walls and the partial reconstruction of the ruins. The photo below shows the exterior view of the reconstructed great kiva and in the background is the ruins of the top photo. Note the size of the people walking the ruins. These are also the only ruins named after the builders.

four corners area in haste and some remained behind. Those who moved took the time to seal their homes, the cliff dwellings, and their buildings before departing. Perhaps it was the Pueblos and Navajos who sealed their homes after they too abandoned the ancient

71

sites after the volcanic eruptions in 1000 A.D. History has recorded that after the Aztecs departed, the Pueblos and Aztec descendants that remained in the area occupied these cliff dwellings for hundreds of years as well. They would have replaced the burned logs in the ceilings and buildings. Because of the newer artifacts left by more recent residents, American archaeologists have credited the Pueblos, Navajos, and other tribes with being the original builders of these cliff dwellings. These new residents probably did build, or re-build some of these structures. Scientists taking wood samples of the newer logs replaced by the more recent occupants of these building would have been led to believe these sites were hundreds of years younger than they actually were. Some of these timbers would have been replaced when the new occupants reconstructed the stone buildings that earthquakes had destroyed, and that the "rain of fire" may have burned. We know earthquakes usually precede volcanic eruptions. As the new residents of the abandoned cliff dwellings, the Pueblos and the Navajos probably made repairs and additions to make the buildings habitable again. However, the written history recorded in the Book of the Sun, El Libro del Sol, documents that the original settlers of the four corners area were the Aztec.

The wood beams used to date the structures would only be necessary for construction of a second floor. Single story buildings within a cave or a crevice could have existed for hundreds of years without needing a single wooden beam.

In 1964, during a 5-year study of the Wetherill *Mesa*, the archaeologists found the sites of "27 Indian pueblos" previously undiscovered. Subsequently, twice as many such ancient pueblo sites have been found in the four corners area. Several years ago, when a forest fire in the Mesa Verde National Park, in Colorado cleared the forest and the dense undergrowth, twice as many new cliff dwellings and pueblo sites were uncovered. Yearly, the number of new uncovered cliff dwellings and ancient pueblo sites keep growing. It is estimated that the native population living in the Mesa Verde National Park area may have exceeded 40,000. Similar residential sites existed in Utah, with larger sites in Arizona, and still larger sites in

New México. A conservative estimate of the Aztec population in the four corners area in 502 B.C. is 750,000 to 1,000,000.

The photograph above was taken at Pueblo Bonito National Park of an artistic recreation of what the archaeologists think the ancient ruins of Pueblo Bonito, New México would look like completely restored. This four-story complex of *kivas*, apartments, recreation, and conference centers was, they think, a ceremonial center or maybe a convention center. New scientific research has uncovered that the pueblo is perfectly aligned with the sun, their God.

Pueblo Bonito's northern wall is perfectly aligned with the rising and setting sun on the days of the equinoxes, March 21, September 23, the two annual crossings of the equator by the sun, once in each direction, when the length of the day and night are approximately equal everywhere on Earth. The pathway below the southern wall of the building at the bottom of the picture is perfectly aligned with the winter solstice (shortest daylight of the year) and the summer solstice (longest daylight of the year). On those two days, the sunrises and sunsets (usually December 22 and June 21) are perfectly aligned with this pathway between the two disconnected walls in Pueblo Bonito. Additionally, Pueblo Bonito is perfectly aligned with one of the stars in the Canis Mayor constellation. Other nearby ruins represented stars in the same constellation; all these ruins are perfectly aligned with the constellation. Perhaps this is why the other Aztecs referred to the residents of Pueblo Bonito as *Chichimecas* (Sons of Dogs) because they lived under the Dog constellation. Below is a photograph of the actual ruins as they appear today.

The solar alignment of this pueblo is an amazing engineering achievement. The alignment of the city and its building was accomplished with ancient skills. Almost a thousand years later, the United States government requested a marker be placed on the exact geographical location of the four corners, the spot where the states of Utah, Colorado, New México, and Arizona meet. Qualified surveyors using modern engineering tools completed the survey sometime after 1913, the year of New México's entry into the Union. The government surveyors missed the location of the four corners spot by about 2 miles.

The 18 ½ year moon cycle was studied and apparently documented by the Aztecs. The same pathway in Pueblo Bonito is perfectly aligned with the rising and setting moon at the beginning of each 18 ½ year cycle. This alignment of the outer walls of Pueblo

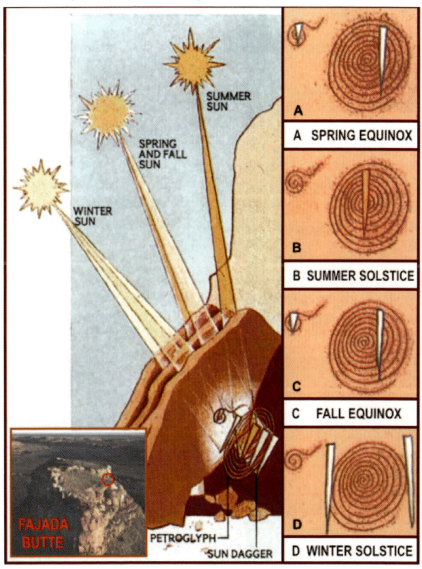

This one of a kind sun-and-moon time-dial was constructed by the Aztec civilization on Fajada Butte, located directly behind Pueblo Bonito, New México. The three sandstone slabs are about 6 and ½ feet high each, and had to be placed at a precise angle, on a precise location, so as to allow the sunlight to cast a dagger of light on the petro glyph. Imagine the know-how needed to construct such a lunar/solar time calendar. Further, during the night the moonlight casts its light on the nine lines on the same petro glyph, which can actually record the 18 ½ years lunar cycle as well.[1]

1   This information was taken from "A Unique Solar Marking Construct," by Anna Sofaer, Volker Zinser, and Rolf M. Sinclair, and the book by Plog (1997/101).

Bonito with the sun and the moon cannot be by accident. The south wall is so perfectly aligned that at noon the northern wall of the pathway casts no shadow. Additionally, this town is also perfectly aligned with true North, South, East and West; plus, one could rightfully conclude that the solar alignment of the pueblo served as a huge sundial (clock) and a yearly calendar as well.

Our ancient ancestors were definitively much better observers of their environment than we are today, probably out of necessity. For example, the winter solstice, December 21, the shortest day of the year, was significant in ancient cultures because winter starts on that day. It was the correct time of the year to make sure you know the amount of food reserves on hand and to decide how these food supplies are to be shared in order to survive the winter. For the Aztecs, at that time period, it was a matter of life or death.

In England, the ancient ruins of Stonehenge were perfectly aligned with the winter solstice sunrise and winter solstice sunset as well. In the mythology of Greeks, "the gods and goddesses met on the winter (December 21) and summer solstice (September 22) and Hades (God of the underworld). They were permitted to enter Mount Olympus only on those two days. The Chinese and other East Asians held their most important festival during the Winter Solstice on or around December 21, when the sunlight is the weakest and daylight shortest. During this festival, it is traditional for families to come together, reuniting, and eating a rice dish that symbolizes reunion.[39]

In Mexican American culture, in December we eat *tamalli*, or *tamales* in Spanish, maize stuffed with meat, wrapped in corn leaves and steam cooked. Usually, *frijoles* (beans) cooked over a very low fire are part of this meal. The *tamales* and *frijoles en bola, con chile*, are ancient meals which Mexicans have been preparing and serving for centuries. When we, Chicanos eat tamales at Christmas, we are continuing a tradition that our ancestors have been practicing in the American Southwest for over 3,300 years.

---

39   Information taken from http://en.wikipedia.org/wki/winter_solstice#Date

The Spring Equinox (March 21) and the Summer Solstice (September 22) were very important to the Aztec. These are the days of the year when the sun is perfectly aligned with the earth's equator. On those two days, there is an equal amount of daylight and nighttime (about 12 hours of each). The spring equinox signals the time to plant, and the summer solstice signals the time to harvest the crops, and to begin the process of drying whatever foods you are going to store, three very important functions to a farming community. Maybe that is why the Native Americans were such keen observers of the skies. It was the difference between having enough food for the winter months or of starving to death.

Based on the recorded history contained in *El Libro del Sol* the Aztecs were the American Natives that resided in the American Southwest since 1386 B.C. They lived in the four corners area for 17 Aztec Calendars (884 years). Today, Mexican American citizens and Chicanos refer to this ancient homeland of the Aztecs as *Aztlán* (the land of the egrets).

American History has failed to record the extraordinary achievements of our ancient ancestors. They were responsible for domesticating and developing a number of foods we consider common today. We should think kindly of these ancestors when we sit down at the dinner table to eat *guajolotl* (*guajolote* in Spanish, turkey in English) on Thanksgiving Day, and by applying genetic selection they also developed useful strains of corns, beans, *potatl* (potatoes), *tomatl* (tomatoes), *xocolatl* (chocolate), and pecan nuts.

Chapter III: Fictitious Native American History

Buried somewhere in federal government warehouses, or in a document storage cave, or in some university library collection of archived documents, there may survive accurate accounts of the history of Native Americans. Accurate histories do exist; our government officials and some American historians have offered reasons for the suppression of these accurate histories.

Too few public schools teach Native American History. Very few educational institutions hire or invite Native American scholars to teach American History. Consequently, when pre-Columbian History, the history of the Native Americans, is taught, the accuracy of the history is highly suspect, and in some cases, outright fictional. For example, in the United States of America one of the fictitious statements commonly taught to our children in most public schools is "Christopher Columbus discovered America." Another perhaps more malicious fictitious statement is that "The American West was a 'wild frontier' that needed to be tamed and settled." These statements were blatant lies[40] when they were taught to me over 60 years ago, and these lies are still being taught to our children today.

We need to stop perpetuating false information to our children such as "When the first Europeans arrived in America, they were greeted by Native Americans who had lived on this continent for thousands of years." As a rule, pre-Columbian history of the Native Americans is seldomly taught to our youngsters. Much can be learned from Native Americans, even a little humor. For example, in 2009, on a tour thru the Grand Canyon the Native American guide stated to the tourists, "The Hopi have been providing guided tours to white people since 1540. That's the year my ancestors gave the Spanish explorer Francisco Vásquez de Coronado and his men the first guided tour of the Grand Canyon and of the American Southwest."

The language of the *Hopi* is in the *Uto-Nahua* or *Uto-Aztecan* family, and as such, they are probably direct descendants of

---

40   I am using the definition of "Lie" given on page 827, by "The Random House Dictionary of the English Language (1966 Unabridged Edition)." The noun definition is: "A false statement made with deliberate intent to deceive; and intentional untruth; a falsehood." The verb definition is: "To express what is false, or convey a false impression."

a Nahuatl-speaking people. To my knowledge, the Hopi Nation is the only American Native Nation, which never, ever signed a treaty with any agency, public or private. Therefore, as a people they are and have always been a sovereign nation. I also hypothesize that the Hopi are direct descendants of the *Nahuatl* – speaking (Aztec) nation that left the area after the volcanic eruptions in the San Juan Mountains, "the Rain of Fire," in the year 502 B.C.

The Hopi are currently living in the 4th Sun. Their first time period ended with "the Rain of Fire," the Aztec's 2nd *Sol*. Consequently, they are probably direct descendants of the Aztecs that remained behind after the main body of the Aztec nation departed after "the Rain of Fire."

A copy of this map, the 1847 Disturnell Map, was attached to the Treaty of Guadalupe-Hidalgo, the Treaty, which ended the Mexican American War of 1846-1848.[41] During the Treaty negotiations this map was used "to negotiate"[42] the new borders for the United States. As a result of the negotiations, the United States aquired México's northern territory, which is now referred to as the American Southwest. US historians refer to these former Mexican territories as having been "annexed."

This map is important for several reasons. It identifies the "*Antigua Residencia de los Aztecas*" – Ancient Homeland of the Aztecs, in several places on the map. Note the rectangle inset with an arrow pointing to the heart of the American Southwest, the four corners area. In the year 1847, and years before, map makers in America and in other nations knew that the Aztecs were the ancient residents of the American Southwest in the four corners area. However, maps made by this company after 1847, intentionally omit this information. Close examination of this map reveals three separate areas clearly identified as "ancient homelands of the Aztecs." Two

41   For more information on this war, read *The Mexican American War of 1846-1848, A Deceitful Smoke Screen* by Humberto Garza.
42   In this case, "to negotiate" is a historical misnomer. A person confronted with an armed enemy which occupies the country and you are unarmed, you certainly do not "negotiate;" not if you want to stay alive.

of these areas are within the American Southwest. One is located between the present day communities of Phoenix and Tucson, Arizona, and the second is further south in the community of Casa Grandes, Chihuahua, México. All three areas are identified as "ancient homelands of the Aztecs" on the Disturnell Map, and all three areas were located on Mexican territory in 1847.

Two other maps produced after 1848 indicate homelands of the Aztec in the American Southwest as well. According to Roberto Rodríguez and Patrisia Gonzales, one of these maps was produced by Robert Montgomery Martin and J. Rapkin in 1851, when these territories were located in the American Southwest. Rodriguez

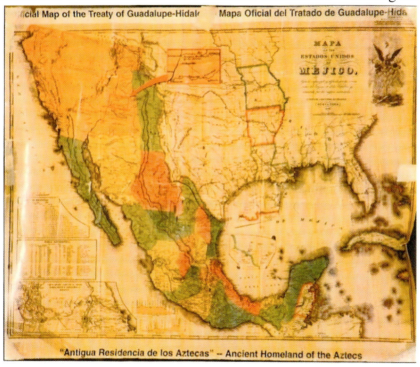

"Antigua Residencia de los Aztecas" -- Ancient Homeland of the Aztecs

This copy of the 1847 Disturnell Map was obtained from Richard Rodríguez more than 20 years ago.
[1] Note the size of Texas, Alta California (brown area), Nuevo México (light green area), and the area identified as the "Antigua Residencia de los Aztecas" (the red outlined rectangle area).

---

1   Roberto Rodriguez and Patrisia Gonzales conducted a very extensive study of old maps, perhaps several hundred maps; some identified the "ancient homeland of the Aztecs." Please refer to their work, "Aztlánahuac: Mesoamerica in North America Exhibit." Or refer to their work, The Story of Maps: Mesoamerica in North America. http://www.sscnet.ucla.edu/chavez/Aztlánahuac/info.htm

and Gonzales go on to state, "Further, this map clearly labels the Rocky Mountains in Colorado as *Sierra* de *Anahuac*. *Anahuac*[43] is the pre-Columbian term for the nation we now know as México."[44] This map also locates Las Casas Grandes Aztec Ruins near Tucson, Arizona. According to research by Rodríguez and Gonzales, the second map was produced by Tallis, and according to Rodríguez and Gonzales, "This map depicts the Sierras de Anahuac in Colorado and shows Las Casas Grandes Aztec Ruins several years after the Mexican American War."[45] Archaeologists who have studied the American Southwest and so badly misnamed the ruins they excavated could have known this information had they studied the old maps.

The first archaeologists who came to the American Southwest used maps, which no longer contained this vital historical information. Consequently, they were unaware that they were studying and excavating in the "ancient homelands of the Aztecs." While they knew these sites were ancient and that Native Americans constructed them, the archaeologists had no clue regarding the correct identity of the builders. Consequently, they applied names they either created, mimicked, or borrowed, and they continue to use these names today such as "*Mesa Verdeans*", "*Chacoans*," "*Anasazi*," "*Hohokam*," "*Mogollon*," "*Fremont*," "*Sinagua*" and "*Salados*."

Scholars in México and in the American Southwest still disagree on the correct location of *Aztlán*, the "original" homeland of the Aztecs. In México, legends and oral history strongly suggest that the Aztecs migrated to *Tenochtitlán* (Mexico City) from somewhere up north, as documented in *La Piedra del Sol;* but how far north is the area of disagreement. Oral history and written legends in México indicate that there were three very important migrations

---

43   In pre-Columbian time México was known as Anahuac . In 1519, according to Dr. Rivas-Salmón Hernán Córtez landed on the coast of Vera Cruz where he was told by the local Natives that the Mejicas up north were the ones who had lots of gold. He told his men, "Vamos a ver esos Mejicanos" (Lets go see those Mexicans.), and thereafter, he referred to this country as "México," and to its residents as Mexicanos. However, we know that Cortes, in his "Letters to Charles V," refers to the Mexica as "Culua" (which appears in various other conquest-era documents; sometimes as "Culhua-Mexica." The only reference from Cortes that comes close to "Mejica" is where he refers to the province or area of "Mesyco," where the city of "Temixtitan" can be found.
44   Rodriguez and Gonzalez (14).
45   Ibid.

into the Valley of Anahuac from "up north." The first migration was made by the *Toltec*, the second by the *Chichimeca*, and third by the Aztec. These three Native Nations were Nahuatl-speaking people, and "all came from up north." I hypothesize that in the distant past (1386 B.C. to about 502 B.C.), the *Toltec*, the *Chichimeca*, and the Aztec were members of the same Native nation. During these discussions of the migrations, it was determined that maps were not used. According to research by Rodriguez and Gonzales, "No maps were used."

These three Native American civilizations, the *Toltec*, the *Chichimeca*, and the Aztec had a written history and took great care to preserve their history, their literature, and the knowledge of their civilizations in codices and in stone carvings. More than a thousand years later, when the Europeans stepped onto the North American continent, they brought "book-burners" with them. These Europeans believed that these ancient texts (*codices*), which they could not even read, contained evil material. Some of these less-than-enlightened Christians professed that the codices were "the work of the devil;" words that provided justification to destroy the recorded knowledge and history of these civilizations. Even the books written on stone were ordered demolished and were shattered into pieces.

History books, as well as other texts such as math books, medical books, and studies on astronomy, political documents, literature, songs, poems, children's stories and myths were destroyed. Every codex the conquering Spaniards could find was thrown into the fire. A few years later, these book-burners sat down and wrote the history of the conquered people. For example; "… Bishop Landa in the community of Mani, Yucatan, exemplifies how after burning all the Mayan books he could find; he sat down and proceeded to write the history of the Mayans."[46]   Hundreds of years after the codices were burned, the new documents written by the "book-burners" are now the "scholarly sources" used by modern historians to write and to teach Native American History.

---

46   Ibid

Baron Alexander von Humboldt (1769 – 1858), a highly esteemed geographer and man of science, visited México in 1803. During his stay in North America, he produced a very famous map, which he entitled, *1803 Map of the Kingdom of Spain*. This map identifies the "First Adobe of the Aztecs," and *Casa Grandes* in the American Southwest. Numerous other maps also identify this area as the ancient residence of the Aztecs, as documented in the research by Rodríguez and Gonzales. The Baron's map is important because he was *"a naturist, a scientific explorer, polyglot, and polymath. He was the last great scientific generalist. Indeed, he believed that no organism or phenomenon could be fully understood in isolation. Living things ... had to be considered in conjunction with data from other fields of research ..."*[47] According to Rodríguez and Gonzáles, his map also *"... depicts the same three immigration points, plus a fourth, more northern one, pointing to Teguayo (the Salt Lake Region in Utah) as the point of departure of ancient Native Americans. Humboldt purportedly made his observations based on ancient pre-Columbian codices."*[48]

Pueblo Bonito, New México, has very little water, and the land is unsuitable for farming. The Pueblo appears to have been built "in the middle of nowhere," in a very bad location, and its location casting doubt on the judgment of the builders. Anna Sofaer, Volker Zinser, and Rolf M Sinclair have taken an inter-disciplinary approach to studying the archaeological evidence at Pueblo Bonito, Chaco Canyon, and the surrounding areas. These archaeologists have made great progress in understanding the significance of this ancient civilization. They have learned that Pueblo Bonito was intentionally constructed at a precise geographical location, and they now understand the significance of the town's main buildings. They are aligned to true North, South, East, and West. The buildings and walls are perfectly aligned with the rotation of the earth, the sun, the 18 ½ year cycle of the moon, and to the sun's solstices and equinoxes. Additionally, Pueblo Bonito, Chaco Canyon, and numerous other ruins are perfectly aligned with a constellation in the sky.

47   http:llwww.lib.utulsa.edu/speccoll/collections/maps/humboldt/index.htm.
48   http://www.burlingtonnews.net/map.html.

Gary A. David, "an independent researcher, poet, archaeo-astronomer"[49] and author of two books (*The Kivas of Heaven, Ancient Hopi Starlore* and *The Orion Zone: Ancient Star Cities of the American Southwest*), discovered that numerous ancient ruins in the American Southwest are perfectly aligned with the constellations Orion, Taurus, Gemini, Canis Minor, Canis Major, and Auriga. The most astonishing to me was the Orion constellation. Each of Orion's stars is perfectly aligned with an ancient ruin. This alignment cannot be by accident. The following chart produced by Gary A. David demonstrates the relationships he clearly establishes between the ruins in the American Southwest (Terra Orion on the left) and the Orion constellation in the sky (Astra Orion on the right) reversed 180 degrees:

David's books are must-read for historians of the American Southwest. Note that the Orion constellation extends toward the Grand Canyon, and that Canyon de Chelly corresponds exactly with the star Saiph, and Wupeki (the Aztec ruins) are at the exact location of the Bellatrix Star in the Orion constellation, and the Orion Belt stars are the 3rd, 2nd, and 1st Mesas (Aztec ruins).[50]

Gary A. David discloses how some of the other constellations mirror the actual locations of Aztec ruins in the American Southwest. The Chaco Meridian provides another example. The 108 degree longitudinal line extending from Mt. Whitney to Chaco Canyon, to the Salmón Ruins, and much further south to Casas Grandes, Chihuahua is perfectly aligned with the stars Mirzan and Sirius. Sirius, the brightest star in the heavens, corresponds to Chaco Canyon in the Canis Major constellation (the constellation of the Dog). David's book contends that, "the Chichimeca (literally Sons of the Dog) lived in Chaco Canyon and perhaps constructed the pueblos there before they migrated southward in the 13th century A.D. to become the Aztecs in the Valley of México."[51] It is interesting to note that the term "*Chichimeca*," a derogatory term used by the indigenous people of Central México to refer to the

49   http://www.theorionzone.com/maps.htm.
50   Paraphrased from the above cited author (Ibid).
51   Ibid.

Northern "barbaric" tribes, could actually be a term referring to the civilizations that built their cities to correspond to the constellation of the dogs (Canis Major and Canis Minor). It is unknown whether the original inhabitants of Chaco Canyon also knew these constellations by similar names, but it is definitely an interesting coincidence worthy of further investigation. Mr. David also believes that "... the *Hopi* and other Pueblo people of the ancient Southwest undoubtedly had contact with the *Maya*, *Toltec*, and Aztec of Mesoamerica."

Researcher James Q Jacobs has documented, "... that Big Horn Medicine Wheel, Aztec Pueblo, the pueblos of Chaco Canyon, and the pueblos in Mimbres Valley are all situated on an approximate north-south line near the 108th meridian (the Chaco

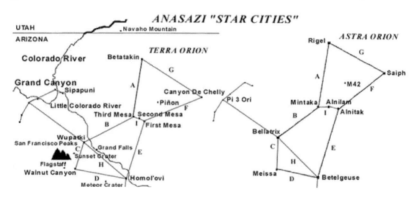

Meridian)."[52] He also noticed that the ruins of Casas Grandes, Chihuahua, México are on the same meridian. In addition, he noticed that the arc distance from Mount Wilson, one of the highest peaks in the Rocky Mountains *(Sierra Anahuac),* to Pueblo Bonito equals exactly 1/200th of the circumference of the earth. I hypothesize that the Aztecs deliberately chose the location of Pueblo Bonito because of this reason. For example, Jacobs also noticed that from the "... *Tenochtitlán* pyramid to the Castillo pyramid at Chichen Itza is 1/36th of circumference distance (10.0 degrees) and that Tikal to Chichen Izta, the arc distance is 1/100th of circumference."[53] Our Native Americans, the ones erroneously labeled "savages," were <u>remarkable mathematicians</u> and excellent observers of the skies.

52   http://www.jqjacobs.net/chaco_meridian.html .
53   Ibid.

Jacobs concluded, "The degree of geospatial intelligence in the ancient Americas was certainly greater than historically known. The sophistication of ancient geodesy and astronomy in prehistory transcends current paradigms in archaeology. Well, reality is transcendental, independent of thought about it. Ignorance of the past not equating to a past of ignorance is no surprise. Geospatial intelligence in the ancient world was apparently far greater than documented by current historians. The telescope is no substitute for counting and thinking."

Patrick King, a graduate student at the University of Utah, Department of Architecture, wrote in his master thesis, "Chaco Canyon depicts the highest degree of specification in the period. Within an area only two miles wide by eight miles long are located ten to twelve major pueblos and many smaller sites. The largest site is Pueblo Bonito, which has over 800 rooms. …The pueblo ruins of Chaco Canyon are noted for their massive walls and excellent masonry. The details of stonework at the corners of walls and at door jambs are of superior workmanship. The masonry of the kivas of Chaco Canyon is of the finest craftsmanship."[54]

Mr. King noted that near each Catholic mission built by the Spanish missionary in New México was a kiva. He believes that, *"The kiva system prolonged the Indian culture. … In every religious ceremony of the Indians there is a period when they enter the kiva to conduct secret ceremonies, which include the devotion of a certain amount of time to the retelling of the history of their clans. By this method their cultural heritage was passed from one generation to the next."*[55]

The Aztec civilization extended throughout the states of New México, Colorado, Utah, Arizona, and Texas, and into the Mexican states of Sonora and Chihuahua. Pueblo Bonito, I hypothesize, was a University, a learning center, where students learned professions such as the priesthood, medicine, diplomacy, writing, astronomy, or

---

54   King, Patrick. 1972. Master Thesis entitled: Pueblo Indian Religious Architecture, University of Utah Library, Salt Lake City, Utah, p. 24.
55   Ibid, p.3.

mathematics; or a trade such as stone masonry, building, farming, crafts and warfare. The small, windowless rooms at Pueblo Bonito were food storage rooms, and the numerous kivas were classrooms. Aztec youngsters learned skills, a trade, or a profession at the *calmecas* (schools). At Pueblo Bonito numerous *kivas* (classrooms) were necessary to accommodate the number of students and the diversity of trades and professions.

Several American archaeologists have referred to the archaeological evidence uncovered in the American Southwest as mysterious and difficult to explain. At times they suspect that civilizations centered in México may have been the builders and occupiers of the sites. They speculate as follows:

… Sun daggers, long distance communications, 30 feet wide roads, which connected most of these villages and towns throughout the Southwest, mammoth buildings… What social system created these ingredients of the Chaco phenomenon? The answer to this great riddle of archaeology runs the gamut of speculation, from space aliens to Natives been the creators of this civilization. Chaco's undoubted contact with México, combined with architectural features common to the two areas, has led many scholars to embrace a hypothesis often referred to as the 'Mexican Connection.'[56]

One study points to the 30-foot-wide roads constructed by the ancient people extending from Utah to Sonora, from Colorado to Chihuahua, across Arizona and New México, linking all the cities and villages. Several sites similar to those in the American Southwest have been uncovered in México, in Casas Grande, Chihuahua, and in the communities of *Trincheras*, *Quibabi*, and H. Caborca, Sonora. These sites contain similar artifacts and petro glyphs as the one seen in New México, the one used to cast a sun dagger. Most of the researchers cited in this work know that this ancient civilization residing in the American Southwest extended well into the present-day northern states of Sonora and Chihuahua, México.

56   Canby, Thomas Y. "The Anasazi Riddles in the Ruins," National Geographic, Volume 162, No. 5, November 1982, p. 585.

Prior to February 2, 1848, the American Southwest was México's northern territory. There was, and still is, a very real Mexican historical connection to these lands and to the ancient residents who resided there.

One of the few books that survived the "book-burners" was the *Libro del Sol* written by the Aztecs. The writing on this history book carved in stone was deciphered in 1965. The *Libro del Sol* indicates that during the 2nd Sun time period (1386 B.C. to 502 B.C.), the ancient homeland of the Aztecs was located north of *Tenochtitlán* (Mexico City), in a place where the soil was red, and four great rivers met. The only geographical location north of Mexico City where four rivers meet and the soil is red, is the area near the confluence of the Green River, the Colorado River, the San Juan River, and the Escalante River. Where these four rivers meet, the soil is red. This is the four corners area of the American Southwest where the Aztecs left their footprints of a highly advanced civilization including cities, roads, canal systems, astrological observatories and training centers.

The *Libro del Sol* was written (carved in stone) in 1479. This historical record claims the American Southwest as the ancient homeland of the Aztecs. The record also documents a prior Aztec homeland during the Aztec's 1st Sol time period (prior to 1386 B.C.) further north, probably in Canada,[57] Montana, or Wyoming (The homeland they remember as their hunting grounds, a time of plenty.).

The Aztec Emperor Axayacatl commissioned the *Libro del Sol* as a historical monument. On its completion it was publicly displayed next to *El Templo Mayor* (the main temple) in the main plaza where all the citizens could read about the historical journey of their ancestors to Tenochtitlán.

---

57   In 1540, Francisco Vásquez de Coronado was exploring the Southwest and when he reached the Gran Teton in the State of Wyoming, he wrote on the top of his map "aca nada" (over here nothing), referring to the vast area north of Wyoming. By the time the map got to Spain, the first "a" had been erased, so "aca nada" became Canada. Gran Teton translated into the English language means (literally) Grand Tit, a large woman's breast. Three years ago when we saw the Gran Teton, it was still shaped like a woman's breast.

Chapter IV: *Maiz*, Corn

As an example of what facilitated the development of an Aztec civilization in the four corners area, we offer one food source, corn. The domestication of *maiz* (corn) by the Aztecs provides an example of their highly developed agricultural skills. The Aztecs as well as other Native nations in ancient México, out of respect, referred to this ancient plant as *tonacáyotl—nuestro sostenimiento—* our sustenance. This one plant, corn, facilitated the establishment of such a civilization in México and in the American Southwest thousands of years ago.

One of the best examples of the incredible ingenuity and intelligence of the native civilizations, which settled this continent is the history of *maíz*. Corn (*zea mays*) is a fully domesticated plant, meaning it cannot reproduce on its own; it requires humans to cultivate and propagate. European botanists (plant scientists) and other scientists were fascinated with corn when it was presented in Europe after the first voyage of Columbus.

I offer the selective breeding practiced by my grandparents as an example of how corn can be cultivated into a very useful product. They were poor farmers who raised their own corn. Harvesting the corn was a family affair. Everyone helped and our parents and grandparents made sure nothing was wasted. The corn stock and leaves were harvested and used as food for the animals. The larger cobs with the biggest corn kernels were set aside for seeds for the following year. All the other corn kernels were fed to the animals or consumed by the family. After hundreds of years of following this simple, but effective process, the small kernels of the teosinte plant became the 16-to-18 inch corncobs we harvest today.

Starting in the 1950's and 1960's, however, botanists began to pay closer attention to corn and to ask where and how it originated. A discovery of fossil corn pollen in the state of Oaxaca thought to be nine thousand years old confirmed that México was the seedbed of corn. In a process that took several thousand years, a wild grass named *teosinte* (which itself produces nothing edible) was selectively bred so as to create the corn we know. The corn we are familiar with today was developed in ancient México. It was an integral factor in the development of the highly advanced civilizations of the Toltec, Olmec, Maya, Aztec, and other native civilizations in México, Central America, and North America.

The Pilgrims would not have survived their first winter without the corn and other foods provided by the local natives. Corn had spread from its origins in southern México over the course of time all the way to the north east portion of North America. As agricultural products such as *tomatl* (tomatoes), *maíz* (corn), and *potatl* (potatoes) spread, so did urban living, calendars, and other advances in civilization.

The significance of corn in Native American culture was not lost on the scribes and priests who created the myths of these lands. In the Mayan sacred text, the *Popol Vuh*, the gods first tried to create humans out of mud, then wood, before turning to white and yellow corn as the material from which to create human beings. The relationship between corn and humans is so fundamentally interwoven into the native cultures of México (in its ancient foods such as *tamalli* (tamales) and *tlascalli* (tortillas)) that it has been described as the foundation of Mexican popular culture. Gustavo Esteva writes in his introduction to a remarkable book on the topic of corn entitled *Sin Maíz no hay País* (Without Corn, there is no Country). He states: *"El maíz es un invento nuestro. Y el maíz, a su vez, nos inventó* (Corn is an invention of ours. And corn, in turn, invented us.)"*.

The people of ancient México also developed a method of preparation that turned it into a complete nutritional food, called *"nixtamalization."* By adding ash or lime (calcium hydroxide) to boiling corn, the grain is transformed into pozol (hominy), which, unlike *elotl* (corncob) or other non-nixtamalized corn, contains vitamin B and all the essential amino acids the human body requires. This chemical transformation could not have happened by accident, as some modern scientists and anthropologists claim. When we take into consideration the fact that this was a food developed by these same people, we begin to understand the incredibly sophisticated chemistry and nutritional science involved in this process.

For example, as corn spread around the globe after 1492, so did a major disease related to its consumption: *pellagra*, "a disease caused by a dietary deficiency of niacin and marked by dermatitis, diarrhea, and disorder of the central nervous system."[58] "It wasn't until the 1940's that modern scientists figured out that corn, in its unprocessed form, is not a complete staple food, and that pellagra is

Note the picture of *teosinte*, the tiny green grass and it very small seeds which was eventually developed, over hundreds of years, into our modern corn. Compare the size of modern corn cobs and kernels with teosinte's seeds. My thanks to Dr. Matt E. Watson for the use of these two pictures.

actually just a vitamin B deficiency that can be corrected by preparing corn in the style of the indigenous people of this continent. What we are saying here is that it took European and American scientists nearly 500 years to figure out that the indigenous civilizations of this continent knew what they were doing when they intentionally added lime or ash and water to the corn before making *pozol* (homimy) or *masa* (dough) for *tamales* and *tortillas*.

In a 1992 essay, University of Massachusetts professor Wal-

---

58   This is an explanation of the term pellagra offered by Thesaurus.

ton Galinat gave a concise summary of the importance of this indig-enous invention, calling the creation of corn "the most remarkable plant breeding accomplishment of all time." In addition, Galinat wrote that corn "has played a crucial role not only in indigenous societies but also in the survival of the first English colonists, in the settlement of the West, and in the rise of the United States as a world power." For a more in-depth account of the accomplish-ments of corn, read Galinat's essay, "*Maize*: Gift From America's First People," in the book From *Chiles* to *Chocolate*. Another great source on this topic is Betty Fussel's excellent book The Story of Corn: America's Quintessential Crop.

Note that corn kernels come in numerous colors. However, the most common colors are yellow and white. In the State of New México some of the residents claim that the darker kernels are healthier and tastier, maybe they are. My thanks to Dr. Matt E. Watson for the use of this photograph.

Fast forwarding to the 21st century: NAFTA, the North American Free Trade Agreement, or *Tratado de Libre Comercio* (TLC), as it is known in México, is an agreement entered into by the United States of America, Canada, and México in 1994. NAFTA, along with our government subsidies to corn growers, has wreaked havoc on corn production in México. The United States government provides more than $10 billion every year in subsidies to corn growers in the United States. Consequently, American farmers are able to sell their product at a price far below what it costs to produce it in México. As a result of "free trade," we have dumped our corn on México, making it impossible for Mexican farmers to compete.[59] Since many of the poorest people in México grow corn, its production serves as a measure of the condition of the most marginalized groups in Mexican society. A 2003 report by the Carnegie Endowment suggests that this 'dumping' has buried an estimated 1.3 million small farmers in México, many of whom end up as economic refugees, "illegal immigrants," in the United States.

In his article "A Flood of U.S. Corn Rips at México," author Michael Pollan writes that it is these very same small corn farmers in México that carry the responsibility of maintaining the genetic diversity of the species. Corn produced in the U.S. is overwhelmingly genetically identical. "This genetic diversity, the product of 10,000 years of human-maize co-evolution, represents some of the most precious and irreplaceable information on Earth, as we were reminded in 1970 when a fungus decimated the American corn crop and genes for resistance were found in a landrace in southern México." The landraces he refers to are ultimately dependent upon the small farmers who cultivate them; the same small farmers who are being wiped out by NAFTA policies are the same small farmers who carry with them the genetic diversity on which the future of the species depends.

Another major issue threatening genetic diversity is the introduction of genetically engineered corn into México. In 2001, the Mexican government discovered that some of the country's native varieties (many in remote areas thought to be pristine) had been contaminated by genetically modified corn. This discovery was all the more alarming because genetically engineered corn had not been approved for cultivation in México. Some researchers believe that this discovery in remote regions is an indication of just how widespread the contamination by genetically engineered crops has

---

59   See Oxfam International's 2003 report: "Dumping Without Borders: How U.S. agricultural policies are destroying the livelihoods of Mexican corn farmers."

become. The pollution of thousands of years of genetic diversity and the economic policies that serve to wipe out that diversity, rob México of its cultural and scientific heritage and throw the entire survival of the species into doubt.

As Pollan points out, "Perhaps from a strictly economic point of view, free trade in a commodity like corn appears eminently rational. But look at the same phenomenon from a biological point of view, and it begins to look woefully shortsighted, if not mad." In just the last 20 years or so, the "Land of *Maíz*" has lost upwards of 90% of their native varieties due to an influx of seed brought by American corporations because of NAFTA. At the same time, México has lost major sectors of its population to Northern migration, making the title of the book referenced above ring even truer: *Sin Maíz no hay País*, Without Corn there is no Country.

Chapter V: A Legend[60]

---

60   This chapter was written by Dr. Matt Espinoza Watson, with minor additions by the author.

Other interpretations of *El Libro del Sol* do exist. The central figure in *El Libro del Sol* represents *Tonatiuh* and the four epochs, or it could also represent the Aztec symbol for movement (*ollin*); or possibly meaning the four great migrations. A dear friend and colleague, Professor Matt Espinoza Watson from Fresno City College, shared his unique interpretation of the "*Calendario Azteca*" for your consideration.

Many people have been fascinated with this image for quite a long time. It's always grabbed, or rather demanded my attention. [61] My pursuit to understand it has taken me up and down the American Southwest and deep into México several times and has cost me a good deal of mental energy. Ultimately, part of what I've learned is that the central figure could be anyone's face; that the symbol you see is universal, meaning it applies to everyone, and that it is also a description of our universe and one of the fundamental principles of life: Movement (*Ollin*) (pronounced oh-leen), and the importance of movement in everyday life, or movement as in a migration of people. Or, for example, it could also be a reminder that without our heart moving blood through our bodies, we would not have life (Not to mention the millions of other movements going on inside our bodies and the universe as well …).

Understanding this symbol of movement and the term *ollin* requires an understanding of the culture that these concepts came from, and the world that shaped them. We must understand also that, as in many cultures, one symbol can represent a great number of things. The symbol *ollin* comes from the *Mexica* or Aztec culture, though the origin of the symbol is much earlier than this civilization. Like many of the people of central México, the *Mexica* spoke *Nahuatl*. In *Nahuatl*, the word *ollin* has as its root in the word *yollotl*, or heart. And so built within the essence of this *Nahuatl* word, *ollin*, movement is the word for our hearts. So when we see this symbol we should see our face and our heart reflected within it. Connecting to the idea on that level is crucial. Whether through movement on a cellular level, our heartbeat, a migration, or the movement of the earth around the sun, we can see the symbol reflecting this funda-

61   Refer to Footnote number 61.

mental principle of life.

As you'll notice, the ollin image from the calendar has four quadrants, which could represent the four chambers of the heart, the four seasons, the four previous world ages (in the *Mexica* worldview), and the four elements that give us life (The jaguar represents the earth (soil); The beak-like face to its left, *ehecatl* (wind), repre-

sents air; the symbol below it in the bottom left is *quiahuitl* (fire-rain), which represents fire, and on the bottom right is atl (water).) And despite what it might seem, we as humans are still dependent upon these four elements for our lives. We are not separate from the rest of the world around us, despite driving around in cars, gazing at screens and living in manufactured environments. We need to be reminded of this sometimes. We are not only dependent on these elements, but they constitute us.

The face in the center of the ollin (from the calendar) was, and in some quarters still is, thought to be *Tonatiuh*, the sun. More recently, however, many others have come to the conclusion that the face may represent *Tlaltecuhtli*, one of the personifications of the earth; this is what is said by many elders from indigenous communities in Central México, where traditional beliefs have been passed on for many generations. I say that "it's your face" not because books or scholars or anyone else has told me so, but because I think that what is represented in this symbol is something that applies to all humans, regardless of where you come from: movement is essential to all of our lives, without movement and mass we would have no gravity, and without gravity we would fly off this planet into endless space. Movement is essential for all life on this planet to survive.

The symbol and the word *ollin*, in addition to referring to the above, is also a representation of another very particular kind of movement...earthquakes. In its simpler form, ollin is blue above red, "like the moment of dusk when the sun is setting and the blue night sky is appearing above the horizon and red fire of the sun.

This is the moment of a great change of energy—this is *ollin*. Ollin is both the masculine and feminine forces coming together. "Ollin is a revolutionary spirit of cleansing, new creations and possibilities."[62] Here, we see the aspect of ollin representing duality, and ultimately balance. Sometimes balance is achieved through earth-shattering means. At times we all need a little (or big) earthquake in our lives to wake us up to the present moment, to ourselves, or to our surroundings.

Another important aspect to consider is that this symbol is the very center of what is commonly called the Aztec Calendar. It is here that we can clearly see that ollin is cyclical in nature. It is

---

62   Maritza Montiel, "The Tonalpoualli: The Heartbeat of our Culture and the Cosmos."

a reminder that life moves in cycles; a straightforward connection with the seasons. Ollin is a reminder to be observant, mindful of ourselves and our surroundings (to watch the way things are moving within and around us), recognizing that at times circumstances around us demand action while at other times, what is best is our disengagement or inaction. If we pay attention to movement, we can learn to act in harmony with what is around us, our family, community, nature, and our universe.

As winter approaches, our surroundings remind us that it is a time of death, of going within, of re-uniting with our families, and we would be wise to embrace that. It is a time to reflect, to look inward and not run away from ourselves, from our subconscious, from our instincts. And when Spring rolls around, we see all around us that it is a time for re-birth, as rain and sunshine combine to make green leaves appear once again, flowers grow, birds nest, animals give birth to off spring, etc. It can also be a time for us to re-invent ourselves; we can try incorporating new habits, make better decisions, or be a better friend. Each spring season brings these possibilities with it, and if we are more conscious of our connection with the seasons of the natural world, we can take advantage of our circumstances.

We are reminded that the world moves in cycles…really long ones and some shorter as charted by our 365-day calendar. The *ollin* image from the Aztec calendar is a representation of the five world ages, the five epochs of the Aztec civilization. According to those who promote a unified perspective of the Mesoamerican calendars, these epochs combine to create a larger cycle of about 26,000 years. It is this larger cycle, a full lap of our earth's wobbling around on its axis; that is completing itself but not really ending in 2012.[63]

In an age when we are starting to understand our history, and we are beginning to awaken to the fact that our planet has a finite amount of resources and a finite limit to the damage we can inflict on it before making it uninhabitable when we are realizing our economy based on continual growth isn't realistic, is it time we look for what else might work? Perhaps it's also time for a reevaluation of how we look at time itself. Are we on a path that is a straight line stretching ever upward and forward, or does time itself follow a circular route? Even if we're skeptical of this radical shift in our view of time, it's clear that we are at a point where we require a reevaluation of how we define American History and "progress" as well.

It has been said before that 'sustainability' and our ecological movements are ultimately rooted in ideas that are indigenous to this continent and that were practiced by many of its inhabitants for millennia. It may come as no surprise then, that the symbol the *Mexica* chose to exemplify the age we live in is movement (ollin).

---

63   This is called the "precession of the equinoxes," and is something that was known by many ancient people, not just in ancient México; for a very in-depth perspective on how this knowledge is encoded into mythology all over the world, see Giorgio de Santillana and Hertha von Dechend's *Hamlet's Mill*, or for a somewhat easier read, check out Joseph Campbell's *The Masks of God*. See www.alignment2012.com for a (relatively) straightforward source on how this topic relates to the Mayan (and Aztec) calendar(s).

Ollin reminds us that in order to move forward, sometimes we must look backward (Learn where we came from; know our history.), understand our past, so that we can then proceed forward with a clear understanding of where we have been. Our history can serve as an effective guide in our striving toward more sustainable practices and our learning about the imminent changes we face in our race to reach our elusive dreams, our pursuit of happiness, and survival.

Some of the people who subscribe to this creative interpretation of the *Libro de Sol* usually believe that:

1) During the 1st epoch, *Ocelotonatiuh*, "lived the giants who were finally attacked and devoured by the Jaguars;"[64]

2) The 2nd epoch was really *"Ehecatl-Tonatiuh*, and that during this epoch the human race was destroyed by high winds and hurricanes, and men were converted into monkeys;"[65]

3) The 3rd epoch was when "everything was destroyed by a rain of lava and fire, and men were converted into birds to survive the catastrophe;"[66]

4) The 4th epoch was represented by the *Chalchiuhtlicue*, water goddess, wife of *Tlaloc* (Rain God) and that destruction came in the form of torrential rains, and during this epoch, men became fish in order not to perish by drowning.

Since the professional translation and interpretation of the *Libro del Sol* by Dr. Cecilio Orozco and Dr. Alfonso Rivas-Salmón, many scholars who first read the inventive interpretation of this history book as written by Charles Phillips and several others have now changed their minds. A few are stubbornly hanging-on to the "creative" but denigrating interpretation of Aztec history. We concur with the scholars who wrote, "The Olmecas and other Mesoameri-

64   García Y Valadés editors, 1995. 16a edition. *Aztec Calendar, History and Symbolism*, S.A. de C.V. Grupo Cultural Especializado, S.A. de C.V., Av. Popocatépetl 510, México D. F. Charles Phillips, *Aztec & Maya*, p.159-161.
65   Ibid.
66   Ibid

can civilizations used critical reasoning to study the cosmos. The search for the truth produced a written system, advanced mathematics, and calendars. The forecasting of the alignment of the stars and planets in the year 2012 was truly phenomenal,"[67] a great accomplishment indeed!

Which interpretation of *El Libro del Sol* appears to you?

The contributions made by Native Americans have influenced the quality of life for numerous Americans of all nationalities. Remember them kindly whenever you eat popcorn, corn on the cob (*maíz*), perhaps their primary contribution to the world. Or maybe we should remember them when we savor a hot cup of chocolate (*xocolatl*), or eat chocolate candy, or a chocolate cake. When you are enjoying French fries, potato chips, or mash potatoes (*potatl*), or when you observe your teenagers chewing gum (*chicle*), you should think kindly of these Native Americans. Think of them when you drive to work comfortably on rubber (*ule*) tires. The indigenous Native Americans and their numerous contributions to the world influence our daily lives more than our textbooks acknowledge. We should give them more credit.

We now share with you an expression common among the Aztecs wishing each other well: *In tlanextia in tonatiuh* (May your sun be brilliant!)!

The End.

---

67   http://us.mg4.mail.yahoo.com/dc/blank.html?bn=570&.intl=us&.lang=en-US

Aztecs in the American Southwest

Questions: Introduction

How old are the human remains that archaeologists found in North America?

What are the two most popular theories of humans coming to North and South America?

What is the Book of the Sun?

According to the Book of the Sun how many years did the Aztecs reside in the four corners area of North America?

Chapter 1:

How many years have Aztec descendants lived in the United States?

What is *el día de la raza*?

What are the dimensions of the Book of the Sun?

Where is the original Book of the Sun located?

When was the Book of the Sun completed?

How did the Aztecs protect the Book of the Sun from the conquerors?

What is the Book of the Sun also known as?

How many suns (epochs) are documented in the Book of the Sun?

Chapter 2.

What year did the Aztec arrive at the four corners area?

Name three standing structures (ruins) that date back to the second sun time period.

What did the Aztecs call the 4 corners area of the United States?

How long the Aztecs reside in the four corners area and what caused them to leave their home site?

Which two scholars deciphered *El Libro del Sol*?

Where was the 3rd home site of the Aztec located?

Which official maps recognized former Aztec territory?

Chapter 3:

What other names are use to identify the former residence of the four corners area?

Chapter 4:

Why was corn so important to the Aztecs?

Chapter 5:

Identify several human movements within your body and state why they are important to you?

What are some of the produce we still use or eat today that were domesticated, or develop by the Aztecs?

Vocabulary:

Aquifer: An underground water source.

Aztlán: The land of the egrets.

Crevices: A narrow opening or fissure in a rock or a wall.

Decipher: To decode so that the contents can be read.

Diversity: Variety, multiformative.

Ehecatl: Wind, the God of wind.

Fictitious: Imaginary, base of fairy tales.

Huehuetlapallan: The old, old, colorful land (the four corners area).

Kiva: A large circular room with a capacity for 500 people or more, which was used for social gatherings, prayer, recreational activities, etc.

Mestizaje: An offspring of two different ethnic groups.

Ollin: Movement, and the 17th day of the month in the Aztec calendar.

Plume: Feather.

Sun: An epoch, a specific time period, which usually lasted more than 800 years and was ended by a natural catastrophe.

Tenochtitlán: Current day Mexico City, the largest and most beautiful city built by the Aztecs on an island in the middle of a lake.

Teosinte: A wild grass found in the State of Oaxaca, which was used to develop corn.

Tonacáyotl: nuestro sostenimiento; our sustenance, referring to zea *mays:* Corn

Tomatl: Tomatoes

Potatl: Potatoes

Tamalli: Tamales

Tlascalli: Tortillas

Nixtamalization: The process of adding ash or lime (calcium hydroxide) to boiling corn, the grain is transformed into pozol (hominy).

Elotl: Corncob

Ollin: Movement

Mexica: Aztec

Ehecatl: Wind
Quiahuitl: Fire Rain
Atl: Water

Bibliography:

Bernal, Ignacio. 1975. Revised Edition, **México Before Cortez, Art, History** and **Legend** (Archor Press/Doubleday: Garden City, New York).

Carrasco, David and Matos, Eduardo Moctezuma. 1992. **Moctezuma's México, Visions of the Aztec World** (University Press of Colorado, Niwot, Colorado).

David, Gary A. 2006. **The Orion Zone: Ancient Star Cities of the American Southwest** (Adventures Unlimited Press: Kempton, Ill).

2010. **The Kivas of Heaven, Ancient Hopi Starlore** (Adventures Unlimited Press: Kempton, Ill).

García Y Valadés, Editors, 1995. 16a edicion. **Aztec Calendar, History and Symbolism,** *S.A. de C.V. Grupo Cultural Especializado, S.A. de C.V., Av. Popocatépetl 510, México D. F.* Charles Phillips, **Aztec & Maya**

Gear, Kathleen O'Neal & W. Michael. 1997. **People of the Silence** (Tom Doherty Associates, LLC: New York, NY)

Graeber, Richard B. 1995. **The Aztec Calendar Handbook; Prophecy of the Aztec** (Historical Science Publishing: Los Gatos, California).

National Geographic, 1491, **America Before Columbus**, October, 1991.

Noble, David Grant. 2nd Edition, **Ancient Ruins of the Southwest** (Northland Publishing Company: Flagstaff, AZ), 2000.

Orozco, Cecilio. 1992. 2nd Edition, **The Book of the Sun,**

Tonatiuh, (California State University at Fresno, Fresno, California).

Plog, Stephen. 1997. **Ancient Peoples of the American Southwest** (Thames and Hudson Ltd.: London).

The Metropolitan Museum of Art. 1990. **México, Splendors of Thirty Centuries** (Bulfinch Press: Boston & The Metropolitan Museum of Art: New York).

Weatherford, Jack McIver. 1988. **Indian Givers: How the Indians of the Americas Transformed the World** (Fawcett Columbine, New York).

Wells, Spencer. 2002. **The Journey of Man: A Genetic Odyssey** (Princeton University Press: Princeton & Oxford).

William, Ray A. 1984. **Living the Sky, the Cosmos of the American Indian** (University of Oklahoma Press: Norman, Oklahoma).